MADE IN GOD'S IMAGE

A Study on Our Human Nature

Made In God's Image: A Study On Our Human Nature

ISBN: 978-1-949343-44-1 (paperback)
           978-1-953759-17-7 (hardback)
           978-1-949343-45-8 (eBook)

Printed in the United States of America

Made in God's Image

Image

A Study On Our Human Nature

C. Orville McLeish

HCP

BOOK PUBLISHING

Table of Contents

To those who desire to know the truth about
who they are. . .

Introduction

Many people often argue whether man is tripartite (three in one) or bipartite (two in one). According to the Christian doctrine of immortality, as well as the teachings of Jesus Christ, it is evident that man is a tripartite being. In most cases, man is perceived as a physical being only, which poses great danger. In his desire to satisfy his physical needs, man tends to lose sight of the fact that he is immortal. It is quite sad that most people still live in ignorance or willingly neglect the fact that there is life after death. On their deathbed, I presume they begin to think that, indeed, their bodies were more than just physical.

Additionally, many people today believe that man is composed of only two major components: the body and the spirit. Although the soul and the body are closely related, it is sometimes confusing and challenging to determine the distinction between them. In that case, the conclusion we often make is that the soul and the spirit are the same. The good thing is that the Bible does make a distinction between the two.

Because man is created in the image of God, man is, therefore, considered a triune being. God said, *"Let us make man in Our image."*[1] From the Biblical point of view, God is a Trinity. This is also made clear by Apostle Paul in the benediction that closed 2 Corinthians. He simply said, "The grace of our Lord Jesus Christ, and the love of God and communion of the Holy Spirit, be with you all." And Jesus said, "Go ye and teach all nations and baptize them in the name of the Father, and of the Son and of the Holy Spirit."[2]

The Keyword during creation is the term "Our Image." This means that God was not alone. Most theologians believe He was talking about the trinity. In the same manner, man must also be a trinity. This

---

[1] Genesis 1:26
[2] 2 Corinthians 13:14 & Matthew 28:19

means man has a spiritual nature quite distinct from his physical body. Let us consider the following verses from the Bible that gives evidence of the tripartite (spirit, body, and soul) nature of man. Apostle Paul speaks of the spirit, soul, and body of God being preserved blameless until the coming of Jesus Christ. Secondly, we are told that the word of God is quick, powerful, and sharper than a two-edged sword that pierces through and divides the soul and the spirit and body asunder. This is because it can discern the thoughts and intentions of the heart.

One thing we should beware of is not all Christian denominations teach the Biblical perspectives of the tripartite nature of man. For instance, Jehovah's witnesses erroneously teach that man has no soul. This is not the case, since the Bible specifically emphasizes that man was created a Trinity: soul, spirit, and body. In the same manner, our Eternal God is a Trinity: God the Father, the Son, and the Holy Ghost.

We should remember that the tripartite nature of man is a fundamental part of the image relationship that exists between him and God. It is also important to bear in mind that life is not physical entirely and thus, man is not just a body! Additionally, neither the body, spirit, nor soul by themselves make up the whole man. Man is spirit, body, and soul. We must seriously consider and agree with this before we can understand with any degree of accuracy the subject of life and death.

This book will confine its study/teachings to the tripartite nature of man, his mind, personality, emotions, thoughts, and will and how they function in relation to each other; vis-à-vis, his humanity.

One cannot truly define humanity by what is already known, but to truly see and know what it means to be human is to stand outside time, space, and matter and look at a human being.

~ C. Orville McLeish

Chapter 1
The Tripartite Nature of Man

Paul writes, "Now may the God of peace Himself sanctify you completely, and may your whole spirit, soul, and body be preserved blameless at the coming of our Lord Jesus Christ."[3] Moses wrote, "And the Lord God formed man of the dust of the ground, and breathed into his nostrils the breath of life; and man became a living being (soul)."[4] The living soul is used to describe man. This term simply came from the fact that God breathed life into a creation made of dust. This demonstrates that man is a critical entity who is a three-part being. This is why whatever happens in one part of man affects the other parts. King

---

[3] 1 Thessalonians 5:23
[4] Genesis 2:27

Solomon states that "…the spirit of man will sustain him in sicknesses."[5] Additionally, Solomon also says that a cheerful heart is like good medicine.[6] God is very interested in all three parts of our being — the spirit, soul, and body.

We are told by Luke that Jesus increased in wisdom and stature and in favor with both God and men. In other words, our mental and emotional growth is important in ensuring that our spiritual contact with God and communion with the Holy Ghost is sustained.

It is evident that God is interested in the sanctification of the body, soul, and spirit. For us to become like Jesus, or become the children of the Most High God, we have to allow God's work of sanctification. Sanctification simply begins when the spirit of God is regenerated through new birth. Paul says that most people have their spirits "dead" to God.[7] This is why many people today fail to have an intimate relationship with God to whom, by whom, and for whom are all things. God fills all things. He

---

[5] Proverbs 18:14
[6] Proverbs 17:22
[7] Ephesians 2:2

is the Creator of the universe. This means that He dwells in and outside the universe. God is the ever-expanding principle of all creation.

God is both immanent and transcendent. He is here with us. God dwells within a believer. According to Paul, Jesus Christ lives within us.[8] This truth is indeed marvelous. God dwells in those who have been reconciled to God through faith in the blood of Jesus Christ. Through sanctification, we desire the Holy Spirit and our soul seeks to fulfill these desires, needs, and wants.

Apostle Paul said that the flesh lusts against the spirit, and the spirit against the flesh. This is the case so that we do not do things that we so wish, but the things that the spirit of God requires us to do.[9]

We must understand that the very first key to being successful Christians is to progressively give up our fleshly desires so that we allow the Holy Spirit to retrain our minds. In most cases, this can be a little painful and, based on Biblical teachings, it can lead

---

[8] 1 Corinthians 6:19 | 2 Corinthians 13:5 | Galatians 2:20
[9] See Galatians 5

to an ongoing death. The funny thing is that dying to fleshly desires results in the fruit of peace, which we always crave. This is part of God's plan for his children. However, most Christians deny the will of God and are robbed of the body of Christ, making it quite difficult to allow the spirit of man and that of God to be in communion with one another. Most of us claim that God dwells in us. But the most important question we should ask ourselves is, if this is the case, why is there so little taking place? The truth is that we must offer unto God our spirit, soul, and body. This does not mean our responsibility and will are taken away before God. Each new day is a chance for us to embrace the cross and the experience of the resurrection of Jesus Christ. Through faith and love we are led into this each day.

According to Dr. Tyler, man is body, soul, and spirit. He explains that the role of the body is to sensor the external world while the soul and the spirit sensors the self and spirit world, respectively.[10]

---

10 Daniel Tyler, Be Successful in Your Ministry I – The Doctrine of Man, Series 1 - Lecture 12, International Seminary (Florida) 1.

This means that man is indeed a tripartite being. The spirit part of man represents the consciousness of God, while the soul and the body represent self-consciousness and sense-consciousness, respectively. Therefore, it is right to say that man is a spirit who has a soul which dwells in the body. Adam and Eve, while in the Garden of Eden, were made whole and perfect through the spirit, soul, and body, but this was corrupted by their sin against God's will. The entire human race is affected by Adam's sin, as it inherited the Adamic sinful nature.[11]

The Adamic nature is always in conflict with the will of God. You might be wondering, so what is this Adamic nature anyway? Well, this simply refers to the inclination and tendency of man to always deviate from the will of God, thus, making the wrong choices. But this was not the end because Jesus came to seek that which was lost and save us.

When one is born again, salvation plays an important role in transforming their spirit from

---

11 Combs, William W. "Does the Believer Have One Nature or Two?." *Detroit Baptist Seminary Journal* 2 (1997): 81-103.

death to life in Christ Jesus. This is evident from the word of God, which states that if anyone is in Christ Jesus, they are made a new creation and behold, the old is passed and the new has come.[12] Pastor, Dr. Creflo Dollar gives further insight, stating that as a born again Christian, we are imparted by the nature of God. This means that we take on the DNA of our Most High God.[13]

Paul says we can stop being unregenerate and we wear the true nature of God in His image, righteousness, and holiness.[14] Moreover, once we are born again, our spirit is sealed to preserve our righteousness, thus, creating a strong barrier meant to prevent sin from ever getting in.[15] However, we are continually asked to renew our minds because our soul and mind still have the residue of sin from the Adamic nature. This is because our thought process was that of the former self and thus, upon salvation, we should first renew our minds. This is

---

[12] See 2 Corinthians 5:17

[13] Jimmie L. Chapman, *Reborn and Transformed* (Bible Believers Books, 2011), 118.

[14] See Ephesians 2:24
[15] Ephesians 1:13

not something that you do once and is final. No, it is a process that is ongoing and we must do this daily through meditation of God's word. This is also how we put on the new man.

Apostle Peter says, "Beloved, I beg you as sojourners and pilgrims, abstain from fleshly lusts which war against the soul."[16] The main reason he said this was because there is a constant battle within the mind. Believers should know that once they are born again, they are made a new creation and are one with Christ, even though the temptation to sin is still there.

It is important for us to understand that in the tripartite nature of man, it is the spirit man's role to influence the soul so that the soul can in turn positively influence the body. Though born-again Christians are redeemed by the blood of Jesus Christ, they are still prone to temptation. Even though temptation is real, it is not sin. It is only actualized as sin when we allow our thoughts, actions, or words to yield to the temptation. At this moment a body of flesh is created, which perpetually craves a

[16] 1 Peter 2:11

repetition of the sin it once partook of. It is this flesh that needs to die.

The Bible reminds us time and again that whenever sin confronts us, we have the power to overcome. This is through the authority, help, and grace of the Holy Ghost. This simply means that there is no way a Christian can live a Godly life without the help of God. We must remember that God gives us strength to get up and press forward in faith even when we stumble in our walk. King Solomon wrote that a righteous man may fall seven times but still rise up.[17] In this case, the righteous man simply refers to a born-again believer in Christ Jesus.

You might be wondering, how then does a believer rise up after falling? Well, our victory over sin is derived from the blood of the Son of God. The power and the presence of the Holy Ghost, as well as our ability to rely on the word of God, is the key to overcoming every situation. We have a guarantee that sin will no longer hold us back. John says, "Whoever has been born of God does not sin, for His

---

[17] Proverbs 24:16

seed remains in him; and he cannot sin, because he has been born of God."[18]

The above Scripture does not say that the followers of Jesus will never sin. No, it simply means that through the blood of Jesus and the help of the Holy Spirit, we have spiritual confidence that our way of life is not characterized by sin. However, some people claim that they are born again but their character does not at all reflect the life and character of Jesus Christ. In such a case, the person may not be born again at all. This might be hard to understand, but it is crystal clear in the writings of Apostle John.[19]

Man as Spirit

The Holy Spirit is the name of the third person of the Trinity. Whenever the Bible refers to Holy Spirit, it is always with a capital "S." The instances where the spirit is referred to with a small letter could be referring to the spirit of man that is a part of his tripartite nature or another spirit. We are going to

---

[18] 1 John 3:9
[19] See 1 John 3:9

focus only on the spirit as it relates to one of the constituents of man.

According to Dr. Clarence Larkin's *Rightly Dividing the Word* (page 86), there are several ways in which the threefold nature of man can be illustrated, using three circles: the outer, middle, and inner circle.[20]

The outer circle represents the body of man, the middle represents the soul, and the inner represents the spirit. This is also how Moses designed the tabernacle, according to the model God gave him. Dr. Clarence continues to explain that the outer part of the circle is the part of man in contact with the material world through man's common sense of touch, smell, taste, hearing, and sight. On the other hand, the middle part, which is the soul of man, is the part that represents his imaginations, memory, conscience, affection as well as reason. Finally, the inner part of the circle, which is the spirit, receives the impressions (sight, smell, taste, feelings and sounds) of the body, which is in contact with the material world. This is the part that represents such

20 Santini, Michael T., Systematic Theology III—Dr Bryan Burton, and Miguel Romero TA. "Dispensationalism and the Soteriology of Charles C. Ryrie."

faculties as faith, reverence, prayer, hope, worship, and praise.

The spirit of man was illuminated from heaven in its unfallen state. However, once humanity fell in Adam, the sin of man shut the window of the spirit. It simply pulled the curtains down and the chamber of the spirit was then taken over by death. Therefore, the unregenerate heart can only come to life when the life and light of the Holy Spirit floods that chamber through acceptance of Jesus Christ. The spirit of man is the sphere in which the conscience of God lives and is the office in which regeneration takes place.

According to Dr. Graham, the main theatre of the Holy Spirit and the part of man's nature the Holy Spirit has affinity to is the spirit of man. Apostle Paul quoted the Prophet Isaiah saying it is written that no eye has seen, nor ear heard, neither in the heart of man entered the things that God has prepared for those that love Him. Many people often stop at this point. However, Paul continues to say that God has revealed all these things to the Holy Spirit, because the spirit searches all things, including the deeper things of God. [21]

According to Paul, man only knows the things of man by the spirit of man within him. In the same way, no man knows the things of God, except the Spirit of God. But then Paul concludes that "...we have the mind of Christ." We have access to God's mind by His Spirit.[22]

In man's unregenerate state, he knows the things of man simply through the "operator of man" that is within him. Our human spirit is only limited to the things of man. Therefore, if we wish to know about the things of God, our unregenerated spirit does not permit us to. Paul explains that the natural man does not receive the things of the spirit of God because he perceives them as foolishness. Because of this, we cannot know the things of God since they are spiritually discerned.[23]

Essentially, the spirit of man needs regeneration before it can comprehend the things of God. This

---

[21] Yorke, M. (2000). *Eric Gill: man of flesh and spirit*. Tauris Parke Paperbacks.
[22] See 1 Corinthians 2:9-11
[23] See 1 Corinthians 2:14

means that man's spiritual nature requires renewal before he can understand Godliness. There is only one thing that stands between man's spirit and Godliness—the will of man. When his will is truly and wholly surrendered to God, the Holy Ghost takes control of man's abode. Once this transaction occurs, Apostle Paul says we will know it. The Holy Spirit Himself will bear witness with our spirit that indeed we are the sons of God.[24]

Unfortunately, many people today, even after knowing the truth, still confess that they get nothing from the Bible. This could be because they are unaware that they need to be regenerated and yield their will to the Holy Spirit of God. This is to ensure that they renew their spiritual man to God. If we are to understand the things of God, we first must accept Him through His Son, Jesus Christ. According to Apostle Matthew, we are not to give to the dogs the holy things nor cast our pearls to the pigs.[25]

We must understand that the spirit of unregenerate man does not have the power nor the capacity to appreciate God's will and works. He is like a dog

---

[24] See Romans 8:16
[25] See Matthew 7:6

that fails to appreciate the holy things or a hog that fails to appreciate genuine pearl necklaces. Peter says that dogs often turn to feed on their own vomit and the washed pig returns to their wallowing in the mire.[26] The dog is simply a dog and the pig just a pig. No amount of religion can cause a change in unregenerate man's spirit.

Dr. Campbell Morgan says that if we allow men of material possessions and the wisdom of the world to touch the things of God, out of pity and false charity, they will simply turn and rend us.

John writes that the things born of the flesh are flesh and the things born of the Spirit are Spirit.[27] Therefore, the things of God and the ministry of Christ's church cannot be entrusted to a man that is not born again. There is a spirit in man, the understanding of which is inspired by God. This is contrary to what the materialists tell us. They simply say that the spirit of man is the air that he breathes. They continue to argue that the body of man is meant for his personality. The spirit of man is his personality, which differentiates him from lower

[26] 2 Peter 2:22
[27] John 3:6

animals. But if the spirit means breath, then there is no way God would have dealt with it as a personality.[28]

God is referred to as the God of the spirits of all flesh[29] as well as the Father of Spirits.[30] Christians can serve and worship God by the spirit. John says that God is a Spirit and those who worship Him must do so in spirit and in truth.[31] In other words, He was saying that man has a spirit.

Man as Soul

We often think man has a living soul. but the truth is that man IS a living soul. Moses wrote that the Lord God created man from dust of the ground and then breathed life into his nostrils.[32] This marked the beginning of man as a living soul. The most important thing is for us to ensure that we do not confound that which is spiritual and things that are merely physical or soulish.

---

28 Clines, D. J. (1968). The image of God in man. *Tyndale Bulletin, 19*(53), 103.
29 See Numbers 16:22
30 See Hebrews 12:9
31 John 4:24
32 Genesis 2:7

Man has a spirit, and the spirit of man serves as a fundamental sphere of activity where spirits operate. This is where the enemy tries to make his appeal to the affection and feelings of man. This simply means that devils don't care whether man attends church or not. All that matters to devils is that the spirit of man does not come in close contact with the Holy Spirit of God.[33]

Personally, I think that devils prefer man attending a modernistic or traditional church rather than practicing prostitution. It is the soul that serves as the seat of passion, desires, and feelings. Hamor said to Jacob that the soul of his son Shechem longs for Jacob's daughter.[34] Additionally, the soul of Jonathan was knit with the soul of David and that was why Jonathan loved him as though he was his own soul.[35] It is evident that man's soul is the site of his affection. Therefore, in the same manner the soul loves, so does it also hate. Therefore, it is the soul where fleshly lusts and desires as well as appetites are stirred up.

---

33 Tozer, A. W. (2008). *Man the Dwelling Place of God: What it Means to Have Christ Living in You*. Moody Publishers.
34 See Genesis 34:8
35 1 Samuel 18:1

We are asked to stay away from the lusts of the flesh that simply cause war against the soul. Additionally, King Solomon says that cold waters to a thirsty soul is like the good news that come from a far country.[36] Isaiah says that it shall be like when a man dreams and then wakes and finds his soul empty; or when a man that is thirsty dreams and then drinks but wakes up and finds himself faint and his soul is full of appetite.[37] The soul of man, which is his affection and desires, is often not directed toward God unless the spirit is regenerated. Man must be born again for him to love God and the things of God. We may have a conscience that is troubled or stirred up emotionally and causes us to go through pain and bitterness, but still we remain dead in sin and transgressions.

This is the point when we feel that we are not guilty whenever we pass judgment on others. This is why others can heed an altar call and shed tears and still they are not born again. Only when man realizes his sinful nature and accepts the grace of God in salvation does he turn his desires and affection to

---

[36] Proverbs 25:25
[37] Isaiah 29:8

God. Once the spirit of God illuminates man's spirit with divine life and light, man starts to surrender his affections and understanding to God.

The virgin Mary said that her soul magnifies the Lord and that her spirit rejoices in her savior.[38] In other words, there was no way Mary would extol the Lord in her sorrow without recognizing God in her spirit as her savior. This means that the very triumph is in the spirit through acknowledging Jesus as our personal savior. In the Psalms, David sings that the Lord restores his soul. The term "restore" in Hebrew means turning back. At no time had David lost his salvation. However, there were instances when his affection and desires were against God's will, such as when he sinned with Bathsheba. He testified that despite all the sins he had committed, the Lord restored his soul. In other words, as Christians enjoying communion with Christ, we ought to bless the Lord with our souls and all that is within us; bless his Holy name.[39]

The soul of man is also the connecting principle between heaven and earth. It is a channel that all that

[38] See Luke 1:46-47
[39] Psalm 103:1

is heavenly passes through to manifest in the earth. Our level of manifestations depends on our level of maturity. It is the soul that Paul is referring to in his discourse about babes desiring sincere milk. He admonishes us to grow up, thereby increasing our capacity to manifest God on earth. My mentor, Dr. Adonijah O. Ogbonnaya, has some excellent teachings on the soul of man. You can visit his website at www.aactev8.com for more.

Man as Body

Nothing could be more absurd than to despise the body and yet yearn for its resurrection.
~ Wendell Berry

The body of man, together with the five senses, is essential in connecting with the physical world. Man's outer frame is in contact with the physical world, and this translates to the way God provides for man and his existence. Without God's help and provision, man cannot exist in the material world.[40]

---

40 Wilkinson, R. (2001). *Rudolf Steiner: An Introduction to His Spiritual Worldview, Anthroposophy*. Temple Lodge Publishing.

Originally, God created man to be pure and undefiled. However, due to the fall of man, the nature of his outer body changed and was transformed into the flesh that is characterized by lust. This is why Apostle Paul says the body of man is corrupted, yet it is has value. He continues to say, "For I know that in me, that is, in my flesh, nothing good dwells."[41]

The Apostle Paul refers to the body as "the outer man."[42] It is, essentially, a man's external dimension. Through the body, man gathers information about the world and is able to relate to it. God created the body, and it was good and holy. Some may think the body is evil, but nothing about the body itself is evil. The evil is man's attempt to satisfy himself by living exclusively for the pleasures of the body, which is considered fleshly.[43] It is living on an animal's level, which is completely dominated by natural impulses, desires, and instincts. When an animal is hungry, it will inevitably seek food. When it is thirsty, it will inevitably seek something to

---

[41] Romans 7:8
[42] 2 Corinthians 4:16
[43] See 1 Peter 2:11

drink. When any urge whatsoever comes upon an animal, it will not fail to try to satisfy that urge.

If we judge another merely by external appearances, we "judge according to the flesh."[44] The Word of God became flesh to save us from being slaves to the flesh and to condemn sin in the flesh. When we participate in baptism, we receive the Holy Spirit and our bodies become temples of the Spirit.

The Bible speaks about the sower who went about sowing seeds on different kinds of ground. There is a spiritual significance to each area where the seed falls. The seed that fell among thorns was interpreted by Jesus to be those who heard the Word but are "choked by the cares and riches and pleasures of life."[45] This "life" is also denoted in its external aspects.

The original word for "life" (*bíos*) is also seen in the well-known story about the Prodigal Son. The Father of the prodigal son divides his "living" (same original word) between his two sons.[46] We also see

---

[44] John 8:15 | 2 Corinthians 1:12
[45] Luke 8:14
[46] See Luke 15:12,30

this same word in the story of the widow who puts her two copper coins in the temple treasury. The Bible says she gave her "whole living (*bíos*)."[47]

Paul also reminds Timothy that a good soldier should not get entangled in the affairs of civilian life.[48] The man who has the goods of this life (*bíos*) is exhorted to share with his brothers who are in need. The "pride of life" spoken about by John seems to be arrogance about one's own resources and possessions. The challenge for believers is not to hold on too tightly to material possessions. The only physical thing in this world that has eternal value is the body of man.

The body of a man is vitally as important as all the other dimensions of his being. It is believed that the body is the last part of man to be redeemed, or to use a more Biblical phrase, to be "transfigured." The idea here is that the transformation Jesus demonstrated before His three trusted companions is the future experience for all believers. That is what Paul is referring to when He said we will all be changed; from corrupt to incorruptibility and from

---

[47] See Mark 12:44
[48] 2 Timothy 2:4

mortal to immortality. It takes place in the blink of an eye, and there is no Scripture that supports the fact that one has to die a physical death first.

The Holy Spirit is also given to the body of believers, which suggest that there is a transforming principle at work within our bodies. We must love our body, care for it, and treat it well because it is one of the greatest technologies on earth. No scientist or doctor can claim to know everything there is to know about the body, and its functionality, and there is much much more to know. The body bears the fingerprint of God because He formed it with His own hands. He knitted the body in the mother's womb. Let us now throw out every doctrine and belief that says the body is worthless and good for nothing because that is far from the truth. Love your body until it transforms into what it was intended to be.

Chapter 2
The Spirit of Man

The spirit man is considered as the consciousness of God and is perpetually open to Him. We are speaking here of what scholars have called the "superior portion of the soul." This is where humanity enters into the domain of the "supernatural." The core of a man is spirit, which is the deepest dimension of his being. Apostle Paul describes this as, "the inner" or "interior man." As André Derville points out, the interior of man, in his most deep personal interiority, is where, as Paul states, the regenerating Spirit moves him, where Christ dwells through faith and where the love that comes from Christ is born. It is simply a question of that secret and intimate part of man, the spirit which is open to God.

The mere fact that man has a spiritual dimension is because he has a human spirit (the "breath of God" in him), which enables him to become a living being, or, as some translations would say "a living soul." The spirit of man is the ultimate principle of a man's life. When the spirit (or the Ruach of God) is breathed into the body of a human being, life begins. When that same spirit leaves the body, death occurs.

A man's spirit is the core of his being and is deeper than his consciousness, intellect, imagination, emotional sensations, and pleasures. It is in a man's spirit and soul that he is most specifically "in the image and likeness of God." Essentially, if a man is living exclusively on the body-level, he will fail to be conscious of his spirit or the spiritual dimension of reality. There are suggestions that the soul has the capacity to overpower the spirit. However, if one opens himself to the Word of God, it can pierce "to the division of soul and spirit."[49] He will discover a more profound level of existence than he ever knew possible.

---

[49] Hebrews 4:12

But as it is written: "Eye has not seen, nor ear heard, nor have entered into the heart of man the things which God has prepared for those who love Him." [50]

In essence, a man's spirit becomes his "contact-point" with God.

"Man's spirit, his *pneuma*," says Tresmontant, "is that within him which permits an encounter with the *Pneûma* of God." It is his built-in orientation to God which instinctively reaches up (*supra*) to Him. It echoes the voice of God first of all in man's conscience. Bishop Kallistos of Diocleia helpfully contrasts the ways of knowing which correspond with these three planes of existence. Body, soul, and spirit each have their special way of knowing: the body, through the five senses; the soul, through intellectual reasoning; the spirit, through the conscience, through a mystical perception that transcends man's ordinary rational processes. [51]

---

[50] 1 Corinthians 2:9

[51] Underhill, E. (2015). *Mysticism: A Study in the Nature and Development of Man's Spiritual Consciousness* (Vol. 8). Aeterna Press.

God may not communicate with a man directly through his body or even through his mind. God is Spirit, so He communicates Spirit to spirit. Paul says it best, "When we cry, 'Abba! Father,' it is the Spirit himself bearing witness with our spirit that we are children of God."[52] Through our spirit, we can perceive and respond to divine realities. Through our spirit, we can discern motives. Some have attempted to describe this function of the spirit as intuition or discernment, concluding that the spiritual man lives in profound communion with God. It is God who "judges all things, but is himself to be judged by no one."[53]

If a man's spirit is his "contact-point" with God, or his built-in orientation to God, then it is only at this level that genuine prayer can take place. Jesus said to a Samaritan woman, "God is spirit, and those who worship him must worship in spirit and truth."[54] The spirit was created for perpetual communion with God. It is at this place that God infuses grace into our being. What is infused in the spirit man is supposed to permeate from there and

---

[52] Romans 8:15-16
[53] 1 Corinthians 2:15
[54] John 4:23-24

enter into our souls and even our bodies. This is precisely how miracles take place. A good example in Scripture is the paralytic man. Jesus first healed him in spirit—forgiven— and then he healed him in body.

Indeed, God has created the human being to be the abode of his Holy Spirit. As the Protestant exegete Henry Barclay Swete neatly put it at the beginning of this century: "The human spirit lies dormant and powerless till it has been awakened and enabled by the Spirit of God."[55]

When we participate in Baptism, an awakening and enabling takes place. Theologian Father Most makes a profound distinction between the "spirit level," the "body," and "soul planes of existence." He writes:

> Man acting in the animal manner has blind impulse for his guide; man acting in the human manner has reason for his guide (with perhaps the help of the infused virtues and actual graces); man acting in the superhuman

---

55 Bolman, L. G., & Deal, T. E. (2011). *Leading with soul: An uncommon journey of spirit* (Vol. 381). John Wiley & Sons.

manner has the Holy Spirit Himself as his guide. It is obvious that with such a guide, the soul can be led to levels far higher than those to which reason would have brought it. Père Bouyer continues to elucidate the relationship of Holy Spirit to human spirit thus: The more the Spirit is integrated with man, the more man himself may be said to become "spirit." As his soul (*psyché*) vivifies his body (*sôma*), it is itself vivified by the Spirit; it becomes "spirit." [56]

Note that in Ezekiel's prophecy, the Lord first promises to give the house of Israel "a new spirit" and then promises to give them His [Holy] Spirit. Those who are baptized are temples of the Holy Spirit precisely because the Holy Spirit dwells in them. Hence to be "in the spirit" means to be living on the spiritual plane and to be completely disposed to the action of the Holy Spirit. The New Testament term for the life of the spirit is *zoé*. It is a term used with special impact in the Gospel of John in which

---

56 Calkins, A. B. (1990). The Tripartite Biblical Vision of Man: A Key to the Christian Life. *Doctor Communis*, 43(2), 135-159.

Jesus identifies himself as the life (*zoé*). Jesus has this kind of life in Himself because He has received it from the Father and He shares this life with all who believe in Him. Jesus' very words are spirit and life.[57]

The Greek word *zoé* is resurrection life. It was imparted and spoken by Jesus, who is referred to in Scripture as the second Adam. The first Adam was earthly, and the second Adam (Jesus) "became a life-giving spirit."[58] *Zoé* is grace life; it is a spring of living water welling up to eternal life. This is the life of heaven beginning here on earth. It is the very essence of "realized eschatology." It allows us to participate in God's life and nature, originating first in Baptism and continues on into the world to come. It is referred to as "eternal life" because it is the life of the spirit, and it will never have an end.

Jesus makes a striking comment that manifests the difference between the life of the soul and the life of the spirit, between super-nature and nature. It is the

57 Köstenberger, A. J. (2002). *Encountering John: The gospel in historical, literary, and theological perspective.* Baker Academic.
58 I Corinthians 15:45)

word *logion,* which speaks of the necessary death of the grain of wheat: "He who loves his life (*psyché*) loses it, and he who hates his life (*psyché*) in this world will keep it for eternal life (*zoé*)."[59]

The distinction between soul and spirit is crucial for leading the Christian life in its fullness and the art of discernment of spirits. The problem in dealing with much theological and spiritual literature on this topic is that the terminology is fluid and, in different epochs and even different authors from the same period, different terms are used to represent the biblical terms "soul" and "spirit." Commonly among scholastic philosophers and theologians, a distinction is made between the inferior and superior portions of the soul (the former representing the soul and the latter the spirit). Dom Anscar Vonier, former Abbot of Buckfast, makes a helpful distinction between the spirit and soul levels of existence while retaining the traditional Scholastic terminology. [60]

---

[59] 2 John 12:25)

60 Vonier, A. (2002). *A Key to the Doctrine of the Eucharist.* Wipf and Stock Publishers.

Generally speaking, it can be said that a soul is not a spirit, and a spirit is not a soul. The human soul is the only exception to this. Speaking quite universally, how the spirit functions is forever in direct contrast to how the soul functions. The spiritual substance we call the human soul has both spirit-functions and soul-functions, but it functions through different parts of itself, or rather through differing powers of the spiritual substance.

Another helpful insight from the same author is that these three biblical dimensions of man as we have outlined them place man at the mid-point in the hierarchy of being. His body has the characteristics of animal life. His spirit has the characteristics of angelic life. His soul is the dimension which is unique to himself; through it he reaches down to the world of animals and matter below him and up to the world of angels and God above him. In this sense he characterizes the human soul as "entirely and exclusively the spirit of the physical universe." In a general audience just before Christmas 1988, Pope John Paul II spoke very effectively about the dimensions of life, which we have tried to sketch above without using the technical New Testament terminology: "Who could ever have thought that we, poor fragile creatures, often incapable of taking care of and respecting even our physical and natural life, are beings made for a divine and eternal life?" As a corollary, it is interesting to note the many correlations between these three dimensions of our being and the light they shed on various facets of the Church's teaching and the spiritual life. The most explicit employment of the biblical/Pauline terminology of which I am aware in the Roman Rite, for instance, occurs in the blessing of the Oil of the Sick on Holy Thursday." [61]

---

61 Calkins, Arthur Burton. "The Tripartite Biblical Vision of Man: A Key to the Christian Life." *Doctor Communis* 43, no. 2 (1990): 135-159.

Chapter 3
Man's Personality and Temperament

Our Personality

Most people are often confused about the difference between personality and temperaments. Well, both are slightly different from one another. Personality simply refers to a combination of characteristics or features that form a distinctive character of a person. In most cases, personality is something complex. The main reason for this is because it is a fusion of energy, genes, culture, environment, ideas, experiences, and psychological perception of a person. These are the factors that have molded who we are. In turn, they influence the way we think and behave. In most cases, we are free to make choices for the things we desire. However, the natural way the brain functions often arises from the patterns that have been there since our upbringing.

According to Gordon Allport, personality affects humans in at least three ways. First, personality "creates." That is, it acts as a causal factor and includes much more than "colorful" or "interesting" aspects about the person.[62]

Thus, personality creates and defines individual thoughts, attitudes, and behaviors. It drives a large part of behavior and almost certainly affects some religious behaviors. Second, personality exhibits itself through recurring patterns, including those in which we relate to others, God, and self. Because these patterns recur, we can sometimes predict behavior by defining the underlying personality. Thus, based on recurring personality patterns, we can predict how one might relate to God, self, and others. Finally, personality displays itself in all-

---

62 Valsiner, Jaan. *The guided mind: A sociogenetic approach to personality.* Harvard University Press, 1998.

encompassing ways such as behavior, thoughts, feelings, and motives.

Although a comprehensive definition of the self may include more than a personality assessment, personality defines a major part of individuality and personhood. Behavior, thoughts, feelings, and motives define a significant portion of our outward and inward self. Thus, personality impacts spiritual expression, and personality change even defines some aspects of spiritual growth.

In *Personality in Adulthood* (1990, 127), McCrae and Costa, note:

> ...ask not how life's experiences change personality; ask instead how personality gives order, continuity, and predictability to the life course, as well as creating or accommodating change. For the psychologist as well as the aging individual, enduring dispositions form a basis for understanding and guiding emerging lives.

To the extent that enduring dispositions (personality traits) form a basis for guiding emerging lives, these dispositions can affect spiritual growth and formation.

The ability of personality to measure spiritual aspects is not a surprise. God created mankind in His own image, in the image of God He created them; male and female He created them.[63] Thus, the image in which God created humankind arguably includes the basic building blocks (factors) of His personality.

Floderus-Myrhed et al. (1989) demonstrate that genetic factors govern more than 50% of personality. To a large extent, genetic factors cause humans to possess characteristics that seem opposite to those of Christ. The Bible suggests that every person possesses a sinful nature at birth. Paul says, "All have sinned."[64] The original sin represents more than a single event that happened at one instant in history. Instead, it includes humankind's nature (genetic tendency) that drives and causes sinful behavior. Christ is not only concerned about our sinful behaviors, but, more importantly, our inner tendencies and characteristics that cause those

---

[63] Genesis 1:27
[64] Romans 3:23

behaviors. Floderus-Myrhed, et al. (1989) show that all humans possess those genetic characteristics in their core personality at birth. That is, human "nature" to sin is genetic!

Our Temperament

Most of the time, we wonder what temperament defines us. Others often can tell our temperaments by judging our mannerisms and behaviors. However, the most important thing to remember is that the Bible details these temperaments and how various people of God were able to devise an in-depth understanding of the human nature by their behaviors and works. The main goal was to improve the human condition. Focusing on temperaments, this theory could classify people based on their personality features. These basic features form the basis through which their temperaments are defined. Most people often try to make a distinction between one's personality and temperament by simply saying that temperaments are inborn while personalities are adopted as a result of nature and nurture![65]

The key here is that the distinction is not always clear. However, the four well-known categories include: Melancholy, Choleric, Phlegmatic, and Sanguine.

Melancholy

Those with this temperament are known to be introverted and very thoughtful. Their analytical personality craves caution and restraint. They pay attention to details, especially when they are analyzing a problem. Melancholy people are also self-reliant, and they often dedicate themselves fully to the task at hand. They can be very creative, engaging in such activities as art, music, ministry, and healthcare among others. Their main goal is to make an impact and permanently solve the world's problems. They are consummate perfectionists, especially when it comes to aspects of their lives and performances.

---

65 Diener, Ed, and Richard E. Lucas. *11 personality and subjective well-being.* Edited by D. Kahneman, E. Diener, and N. Schwarz. New York, NY: Russell Sage, 1999.

Melancholies often are highly organized, economical, schedule-oriented, clean, neat, and detail-oriented. Whenever they encounter a problem, they can easily identify creative solutions. The sad part, however, is that most melancholies experience deep bouts of depression that stem from deep dissatisfaction, disappointment, hurtful words, or events.

Melancholy personalities love others deeply while holding themselves in contempt. In short, melancholies take life very seriously, which in most instances cause them to feel helpless or even hopeless. They are deeply caring people who make great doctors, nurses, social workers, ministers, and teachers. This comes from a deep sense of what others are going through as well as the internal desire to reach out and help them. Melancholies are often loyal friends.

Several characters in the Bible seem to best fit the characteristics of a Melancholy, for example, Moses and Abraham. Moses always wanted to do things right. He always wanted details of how God intended to help him to lead the people of Israel out of Egypt. He demonstrated the ability to pay close attention to details especially when it came to the Law of God as well as the measurement of the temple down to specific details. At some point, Moses was not sure he could lead the people of Israel, which is why he asked God to find somebody else.

Mary, the mother of Jesus, was another example of melancholy. She was very analytical. This is evident in Luke's writings: Mary kept all these things, pondering them in her heart.[66] "Also, be it done unto me according to all you have said."[67]

Thomas doubted the resurrection of Jesus, so Jesus had to prove to Thomas that He was alive again before Thomas would believe. Esther was also willing to abide by the rules and regulations that governed her position as the Queen. However, even when bending the rules to her advantage, she wanted to make sure it was done correctly. She prayed and carefully pondered how to solve the problem systematically.

---

[66] Luke 2:19
[67] Luke 1:38

Sanguine

This temperament is impulsive and always geared towards seeking pleasure. Most people with this kind of temperament are talkers. Their personalities are expressive in nature. In other words, they often portray such characteristics as being full of desire to influence people while ensuring that they remain enthusiastic. This is especially the case whenever they are expressing excitement, often attracting attention.

Sanguines are very sociable, full of charisma, and generally warm-hearted, jovial, full of optimism, creativity, and compassion. Their life is filled with parties and humor. Their enthusiasm and cheerfulness often attract others with ease, hence their ability to make friends. They inspire others to work and join in the fun. They are often full of energy, and therefore are so spontaneous. Their personality causes them to love the life of luxury, impressing others with luxurious travels around world and indulgence in rich and comfortable lifestyles.

The most unfortunate thing about them is that they are very impulsive and often find it hard to control their cravings. This is why most of them are susceptible to smoking, alcohol and drugs, gambling, and taking risk. Sadly, their susceptibility is stronger when it comes to chemical imbalances, addictions, and mood disorders. They often get bored whenever they are not absorbed by an intriguing adventure. A Sanguine is poor at tolerating boredom. In most cases, they will try their best to avoid monotony and routine work at all costs. Most routine jobs are very boring and annoying to them.

King David and Peter seem to have the traits of a Sanguine. Peter always wanted people to trust him. He was essentially dramatic and took the lead to speak up for the rest of Jesus' disciples. In one instance, he promised he would never forsake Jesus. However, just before dawn, he denied Him three times even though he knew Jesus well.

John Mark started out his mission and ministry well, but sadly, he quit. Additionally, King David, Samson, and Barnabas were attracted to others and were somewhat passive.

58

Ruth was probably a sanguine. This is evident in the way she enticed Naomi to allow her to travel with her. She demonstrated how loyal she was to her family. She was full of adventurous spirit because of her free will to move to a country that was foreign to her.

Choleric

This group of people are essentially full of ambition and leadership qualities. This is one of the strongest temperaments and is why people often refer to it as "Type A" or "doers." They are often well known for self-motivation to accomplish their goals. They are aggressive, passionate, and full of energy. They, therefore, strive hard to instill these values in others. Cholerics desire control and are best at jobs that demand strong control and authority. They can easily make quick decisions because they dedicate their full attention to everything they do. However, Cholerics are the most insensitive of all temperaments.

In most cases, you will find that Cholerics care little about other people's feelings. According to statistics, most of them are born leaders who exude confidence. Naturally, they make brilliant businesspeople who are strong-willed, independent, and self-sufficient, among other values. Instead of having a skewed vision, they choose to see the bigger picture, organize things well, and insist on production even in the face of opposition. They demonstrate a strong ability to make decisions, especially when it involves correcting wrongs whenever they encounter them. They are often systematic in all they do so that they exude confidence and independence rather than being subordinated.

Cholerics are goal oriented and have immaculate focus as they work. They are good at math and engineering, and are very analytical, logical, and pragmatic; they are masters at figuring things out. They are often skeptical and do not trust easily, so they need to investigate facts on their own, relying on their own reasoning and logic. If they are absorbed in something, one should not even bother trying to get their attention. Just like other temperaments, these people have their own downsides. Some of these include the fact that they are bossy, domineering, impatient, hot tempered, ruthless, argumentative, and impetuous.

They also appear to be very domineering over other temperaments, especially Phlegmatics. They set very high standards that portray them as diligent and hard-working. In most cases, they are hard to satisfy and continuously strive for success. It is very hard to find a Choleric woman, but when you do, they are often, strangely, very popular. They have difficulty when it comes to issues such as anger, intolerance, and impatience. This is because they prefer facts in place of emotions.

Cholerics do not have as many friends because of their tendency to fall into deep, sudden depression and mood swings. Apostle Paul, James, Martha, Elijah, and Titus seem to have Choleric temperaments. Paul was left for dead, imprisoned, stoned, forsaken, and forgotten. However, he kept his focus on the high calling of God.

Phlegmatic

This Phlegmatic temperament is characterized by a relaxed and quiet character, ranging from warmly attentive to lazily sluggish. Phlegmatics are also referred to as "the watchers." They are the best at mediation and demonstrate a solid position that desires steadiness. They are, in most cases, females who are easygoing, content with themselves, calm, cool, and collected. They are tolerant of others, well-balanced, full of empathy, and keep their emotions hidden. They are also known to be happily reconciled in life and are not in a hurry. They have many friends because they often stay away from conflict that could possibly ruin their relationships. Although they are peaceful, patient, and adaptable, they are often reluctant and indecisive. When it comes to gathering facts, classifying them, and establishing the correlation between them, they are very competent.

Since they are fearful, indecisive, and hesitant, they often have a compromising nature. Such people often worry about everything. They desire to know the deep feelings of people in their lives so they can establish intimate attachments. They cooperate with others so that their relationship is characterized by distinctive interpersonal harmony. This is why they are popular in preserving family ties and friendships. Therefore, they are mostly described as considerate, charitable, sympathetic, trusting, warm, calm, and relaxed. They demonstrate more consistency, rational, curiosity, and observance, making them brilliant administrators.

Phlegmatic individuals strive for greater self-knowledge, and they seek to contribute to society at large. But, on a negative note, they are often selfish, and self-righteous, with a tendency to judge others easily, resist change, stay uninvolved, dampen enthusiasm, and can be passive-aggressive. To some extent, the Phlegmatic temperament is a neutral temperament. Joseph, Timothy, and Barnabas best fit the characteristics of a Phlegmatic.

Nehemiah followed the status quo. He wanted to uphold good administration skills so that all tasks were accomplished as planned.

Hannah was also very submissive and faithful even though her dreams were not yet fulfilled. In some instances, we are told that she appeared "unstable" during her prayer times in the temple. However, once she was through praying, her reaction to Eli demonstrated that she was very stable.

Chapter 4
The Emotions of Man

How does one define emotion, except that it is a seemingly powerful cosmic force that affects our environment? The scientific definition for emotion is that it is a neural impulse that can move an organism to action, and prompt automatic reactive behavior, that adapts through evolution as what one calls "survival mechanism" that meets a survival need.

Emotions as feelings are expressed primarily through physiological functions, for example, facial expressions and increase heartbeat. They are expressed in behaviors such as crying, aggression, and covering the face with the hands. Emotions are specific manifestations of non-verbal expressions. Emotions can also be positive and negative.

Scripture portrays both human beings and God as having emotions. Human emotions and sentiments are important to the life of faith. Human feelings can be positive or negative and are subject to change and misinterpretation.[68]

There is a huge debate about whether emotions work in conjunction with faith, or independently. While we admit that emotions are central to the human experience of life and reality, we often feel a disconnect between what we feel and what we are believing for.

As Robert Solomon puts it, "We live our lives through our emotions, and it is our emotions that give our lives meaning. What interests or fascinates us, who we love, what angers us, what moves us, what bores us—all of this defines us, gives us character, constitutes who we are."[69]

---

[68] Manser, M. H. (2009). *Dictionary of Bible Themes: The Accessible and Comprehensive Tool for Topical Studies*. London: Martin Manser.
[69] Robert C. Solomon, *True to Our Feelings* (Oxford University Press, 2007), 1.

The main argument is that emotions are not always reliable. We are sometimes overtaken with negative emotions, and very often, our reasoning seems a better alternative to our incessant emotions.

Greek philosophers continue to exert a fair amount of influence on our culture. Plato and Aristotle thought that emotions, especially anger, could be irrational.[70]

Seneca even went so far as to claim that anger, particularly because of its connections to violence, has done more to threaten the survival of humanity than even the deadliest plague.[71]

Every emotion can be honestly expressed to God in prayer. So, essentially, emotions lead us into communion with God. If both sides feel emotions, then surely this adds to the communicative process. In marriage, the greatest line of communication is formed on the foundation of emotions. If we look at examples of prayers in Scripture, they are laced with emotions.

---

[70] Plato, *Republic* 4.14, §439C-D; Aristotle, *Nichomachean Ethics* 7.3.7.
[71] Seneca, *On Anger* 1.1-2, 2.4.1, 3.1.3-6.

We must allow ourselves to feel and find greater value in our identity through our emotions, which also connects us to God, who also feels. We have seen examples of God being annoyed, angry, grieving, and jealous. It is not bad to feel, but it must be expressed through the correct channels and used appropriately to enhance our relationship with others, and with God.

A believer's emotional life is shaped in response to God's character. Emotions such as peace, joy, hope, and love are felt and expressed, knowing God's grace, mercy, love, and faithfulness. God gave emotions to humanity. He inserted them into man's DNA, thereby giving him the capacity to experience life as He experiences it. It is wrong theology to think that emotions are a result of sin. While sin may have opened a man's capacity to feel negatively, the emotional function was always there. Even Jesus, who knew no sin, felt and expressed emotions.

Jesus' Humanity and Emotions

If there is one thing that distinguished Jesus, the Son of God, in the flesh as human, it is emotions. Jesus demonstrated that the capacity to feel is what makes us truly human.

The gospel writers paint their portraits of Jesus using a kaleidoscope of brilliant "emotional" colors. Jesus felt compassion; He was angry, indignant, and consumed with zeal; He was troubled, greatly distressed, very sorrowful, depressed, deeply moved, and grieved; He sighed; He wept and sobbed; He groaned; He was in agony; He was surprised and amazed; He rejoiced greatly and was full of joy; He greatly desired, and He loved.[72]

In our attempt to be more like Jesus, we sometimes forget or overlook the fact that He expressed emotions. Jesus is the epiphany of what it means to be fully human and created in God's image. His emotions were a reflection of the image of God, with no deficiency or distortion. If we compare our own emotions to His, we will become aware of our dire need for transformation, so we become fully human as He is.

---

[72] The Emotions Of Jesus by G. Walter Hansen.
http://www.christianitytoday.com/ct/1997/february3/7t2042.html .
[Accessed on June 25, 2017]

Paul exhorts the Corinthians to gaze upon the glory of God, "with unveiled faces" because we "are being transformed into his likeness with ever increasing glory."[73] This is an admonition to look intently on Jesus until the Holy Spirit begins to transform us into the full image of Christ. Paul demonstrated this emotional transformation when writing to the Philippian Christians. He says, "I long for you with the compassion of Christ."[74] Paul was transformed enough to embody the very emotions of Jesus Christ.

Theologians, for centuries, have argued strongly that God is not moved by emotions. Early Christian apologists, for example Justin Martyr, developed the doctrine of the impassibility of God to distinguish the God of the Bible from pagan gods, who they believed allow emotions to lead them into scandalous behavior. Their intentions were good, because they wanted to emphasize that God did not have mad, shameful passions like the gods of pagan mythology. Zeus, for example, is known for rape and arbitrary vengeance.

---

[73] 2 Corinthians 3:18
[74] Philippians 1:8

70

The question then becomes, "What is God truly like?" I believe Jesus answered this question profoundly when Phillip asked him to "Show us the Father." Jesus responds, "He who has seen me has seen the Father." If Jesus then is the full human embodiment of the Divine "Abba," then His emotions also reflect an essential component of the image of God, and undoubtedly reveals the nature of God. Thus, humans are emotional because God is emotional. Emotions become a channel, a scientific technology even, for knowing who God is, and in turn we come into a better revelation of who we are as beings created in His image.

Compassion

One of the most profound emotions that Jesus expressed throughout His ministry was compassion. The Greek word used for "compassion" speaks of a sensation in the gut, which is where emotions are mostly felt. This is where we get the idea of having "butterflies in the stomach."

Who did Jesus feel compassion for? He had compassion for those in need, for example, a leper, a widow who was about to bury her only son, and two

71

blind men. He also felt compassion when He saw people deprived of food. His compassion was often stirred by spiritual and physical needs. There was even a moment when His heart broke when He observed people who were downcast and distressed, like sheep with no shepherd.[75]

In times alone with God, Jesus gained emotional receptivity and energy. As a result of these moments, His vision was clear, His words were empowered, and His touch cured others. He created bread, restored sight to the blind, cleansed a leper, and raised a widow's dead son. His compassion moved from feelings to actions. His empathy was the effective power behind them.[76]

Anger

We are to be angry, and sin not. Jesus demonstrated this as a possibility for us. Mark records Jesus "looking around with anger" at the religious leaders.

---

[75] Matthew 9:36
[76] The Emotions Of Jesus by G. Walter Hansen.
http://www.christianitytoday.com/ct/1997/february3/7t2042.html .
[Accessed on June 25, 2017]

Jesus' expressions of sinless anger were profound and dramatic throughout His ministry.

Aristotle saw clearly that "anyone can become angry — that is easy. But to be angry with the right person, to the right degree, at the right time, for the right purpose, and in the right way — that is not easy." That is the challenge before us.[77]

The most remarkable demonstration of this was when Jesus entered the temple that was used commercially. He was inflamed with zealous anger that moved Him to violent action. He boldly declared the words of the prophet, "My house shall be called a house of prayer for all nations."[78] G. Walter Hansen wrote, "The pursuit of profits had excluded the opportunity for Gentiles to find and worship God in the court of the Gentiles, where people of different ethnic backgrounds and physically disabled people could gather to worship. But merchants had packed that area with their tables, stalls, boxes, and animals. People who had

---

[77] The Emotions Of Jesus by G. Walter Hansen.
http://www.christianitytoday.com/ct/1997/february3/7t2042.html .
[Accessed on June 25, 2017]
[78] Mark 11:17 | Isaiah 56:7

73

traveled a long way to find God were shut out. Though the terrified merchants running from the crack of his whip saw only the destruction of business as usual, Jesus' anger was motivated by 'zeal for your house' and directed toward the positive purposes of the worship of God and the mission to all nations."

We must not make the mistake of using the temple story to justify wrong behavior, and unforgiving animosity. Paul was very aware of this tendency when he wrote, "Be angry, but do not sin; do not let the sun go down on your anger, and give no opportunity to the devil."[79]

Anger is like a fire. It can be destructive, and harm and destroy a life. But the anger expressed by Jesus within us can warm and restore life.

Grief

One of the shortest verses in the Bible is "Jesus Wept."[80] It is remarkable to read that story, because

---

[79] Ephesians 4:26-27
[80] John 11:35

Jesus knew He was going to raise Lazarus from the dead. It seems a waste of tears to cry at that point, but Jesus demonstrated a universal truth: there will be moments of grief in our lives.

We need to understand that God never truly knew what it meant or felt to be human until He came in human form (Jesus). That is why the Scriptures say, "For we have not an high priest which cannot be touched with the feeling of our infirmities; but was in all points tempted like as *we are, yet* without sin."[81] God experienced all the emotions that Jesus experienced through His victories, suffering, and death.

When Jesus saw Lazarus' sister Mary weeping, "He was greatly disturbed in spirit and deeply moved."[82] The word "disturbed" is used in the context of being in anguish. He groaned in the depths of His spirit.

Jesus also grieved at the betrayal of his friend, Judas. He loved him like all the others and allowed him to participate in everything He did, even knowing Judas would one day betray him. There is a lesson

---

[81] Hebrews 4:15
[82] John 11:33

there for all of us, as we, acting in emotions, are quick to kick people out of our immediate circle due to their short-comings and imperfections.

The most profound expression of emotion was in the garden of Gethsemane where Jesus was mentally preparing for His final night before being hanged on a cross. He says to His disciples, "I am deeply grieved, even to death."[83]

Jesus was very familiar with grief, and we often think that our own experiences of grief signals His absence in our circumstances, but He understands more than we may be willing to accept. The reality is, we want to escape from our emotions and not learn and grow from them or express them to a level that will provoke personal transformation.

Jesus experienced other emotions like joy and love. The intensity of Jesus' emotions is like a mountain river, cascading with clear water. There is an open invitation for us to come and drink, participate in what it truly means to be human.

---

[83] Matthew 26:38

Jesus (being human) shows what God intended us to be as His image-bearers. Jesus' humanity is a perfect humanity, untouched by sin. So in Him, we see what we as Christians will become once and for all, that is, the kind of humanity we will experience for all eternity.

These days, not many people deny the humanity of Jesus. As a matter of fact, most people would prefer to think He was *only* human. That is because the humanity of Jesus is not threatening to anyone. On the other hand, His deity seems threatening, because if Jesus is truly God, we must *submit* to Him, *honor* Him, and *obey* Him, and this is not what sinful people want to do. Nevertheless, both the full humanity *and* deity of Jesus are inseparable from Christianity and our hope of salvation through Him.[84]

Mankind's Emotions

Men are emotional beings. It can be argued that women are more emotion than men, but is this true?

---

[84] Aaron, D. (2012). *Understanding Theology in 15 Minutes a Day* (p. 102). Minneapolis, MN: Bethany House Publishers.

Maybe the truth is that the dominant expressed emotion of the two is different. A man may be more adept in expressing calmness under different circumstances, while a woman is more prone to agitation. But humanity is emotional at its core nature.

Emotions in the Old Testament were generally connected to various body parts—the heart could have emotions and thoughts, while the gut or liver were also of importance for emotions. Smith explains, "Israelites associated emotions with the internal organs where the emotions were perceived to be felt physically" (Smith, "Israelite Emotion," 431). While anger is often associated with a burning of the nostrils, the heart is the center for joy. However, joy does not remain in the heart, but is part of a movement towards appropriate action, explaining the relevance of joy in religious activities (Smith, "Israelite Emotion," 435–36).[85]

---

[85] Heyink, B. (2016). Joy. In J. D. Barry, D. Bomar, D. R. Brown, R. Klippenstein, D. Mangum, C. Sinclair Wolcott, … W. Widder (Eds.), *The Lexham Bible Dictionary*. Bellingham, WA: Lexham Press.

Emotions play an important role in human life. It is believed that a lot of the chaos in our society is a result of human emotions. This would also indicate that a lot of what is right in our society also stems from expressing human emotion, for example, desire. Ben Goertzel, in his article titled, "A General Theory of Emotion in Humans and Other Intelligences" believes that "human emotions are merely one particular manifestation of a more general phenomenon – which must be manifested in some way in any mind." He strongly believes that emotions are directly tied to our mental life, thereby forming the foundation for many psychological issues. He defines emotions as "a mental state that arises spontaneously rather than through conscious effort and is often accompanied by physiological changes; a feeling: the emotions of joy, sorrow, reverence, hate and love."

In the case of human emotions, the "accompaniment with physiological changes" mentioned in the above definition of emotion seems to be a key point. It seems that there is a time lag between certain kinds of broadly-based physiological sensations in the human brain/body, and registration of these sensations in the human brain's virtual multiverse modelers.[86]

Charles Darwin had a theory that emotions are evolved expressions and not purely culturally conditioned. The shared emotions across the globe supports Darwin's idea. While some people believe that emotions are personal, intimate, and private expressions, from an evolutionary understanding, they are impersonal mechanisms that everyone shares.

There is one emotion I would like to address because it is common to all humanity and is a force strong enough to prevent us from becoming who God designed us to be: Fear.

Fear

H.P. Lovecraft penned this famous quote, "The oldest and strongest emotion of mankind is fear, and

---

[86] A General Theory of Emotion In Humans and Other Intelligences by Ben Goertzel.
http://www.goertzel.org/dynapsyc/2004/Emotions.htm. [Accessed on June 25, 2017]

the oldest and strongest kind of fear is fear of the unknown."

Fear is addressed more than three hundred times in Scripture. Each time an angel appears to a human, the first statement is, "Do not be afraid." Paul profoundly addressed this issue as well when he wrote, "For God has not given us a spirit of fear and timidity, but of power, love, and self-discipline."[87]

From an evolutionary perspective, the emotion of fear protected humans from predators and other threats to the survival of the species. So, it is no wonder that certain dangers evoke that emotion, since fear helps protect you and is therefore adaptive, functional, and necessary. However, there is another important aspect of emotions to consider that, in the case of fear, may be important to decision-making as well as survival. That is, when an emotion is triggered, it has an impact on our judgments and choices in situations (Lerner and Keltner, 2001).[88]

---

[87] 2 Timothy 1:7
[88] The Complexity of Fear by Mary C. Lamia.
https://www.psychologytoday.com/blog/intense-emotions-and-

We need to understand that from a Biblical standpoint, the opposite of fear is not faith, but love.

Such love has no fear, because perfect love expels all fear. If we are afraid, it is for fear of punishment, and this shows that we have not fully experienced his perfect love.[89]

Dr. Adonijah O. Ogbonnaya attaches fear to the silver cord that is mentioned by King Solomon. When this silver cord is broken, death occurs. Remarkably, this only now applies to non-believers who have this silver cord still intact. Therefore, if their soul leaves their body without spiritual assistance, and this cord gets broken, they die. A believer does not have a silver cord because Jesus dealt with the issue of death. Indeed, we have not received a spirit of fear. Paul says, don't allow yourself to fall back into bondage to the spirit of fear.[90] You have more reasons to be bold, than to fear. God, who is greater than all, lives in you. If He has made us one with Himself, then there is no more

strong-feelings/201112/the-complexity-fear. [Accessed on June 25, 2017]
[89] 1 John 4:18 - NLT
[90] Romans 8:15

separation. We are not separate from God, except in our consciousness. We cannot be afraid of devils, attributing strength to them, subjecting ourselves to their wiles and mischief and cowering in fear at their presence, and still say God is more powerful than they are. That is an intolerable contradiction. If God is indeed more powerful, then, by definition, so are you. Greater is the one who lives inside you, than anything else that doesn't. So, what is your issue really? Why are you so afraid, really?

Chapter 5
Man's Thoughts

W ith the writings of Paul, one moves into the Greek world. Paul understood the mind as distinct from the spirit of man. It possesses the ability to understand and to reason; it is the seat of intelligence. In other places, mind is used in a broader sense that includes the entire mental and moral process or state of being of a man. A man's actions flow from the inclinations of his mind. Whether a man is good or evil depends on the state of his mind.[91]

---

[91] Elwell, W. A., & Beitzel, B. J. (1988). Mind. In *Baker encyclopedia of the Bible* (Vol. 2, p. 1461). Grand Rapids, MI: Baker Book House.

The mind of man is the seat of thoughts. It becomes clear then, that a man is defined by his thoughts, which determines how he acts and reacts in this world.

All creation began as a thought. Every great invention or technological advancement began as a thought. Thoughts are the origin of our reality. Great architects know that the success of their vocation is dependent heavily on their ability to see what their clients want to manifest. There is no structure, device, or anything material that was not first conceived as a thought. God knows the thoughts and intents of the heart. If we think from our mind, then from a Scriptural perspective, our mind is in our hearts.

The thought life is a mystery from a neuroscientific point of view. It is strongly believed that thoughts are a brain function, but there is no evidence as to how this works. Scientists have tried to determine if neurons are involved in the fabrication of thoughts to figure out if conscious thoughts require an activation of specific networks in the brain regions. It is a mystery, but the fact is that thoughts are powerful.

King Solomon must have recognized this when he said, "For as he thinketh in his heart, so is he."[92] Humanity's existence then becomes a subtotal of his own thoughts. It should not surprise us then that Paul would say, "Fix your thoughts on what is true, and honorable, and right, and pure, and lovely, and admirable. Think about things that are excellent and worthy of praise."[93] Paul is suggesting here that we possess the power to choose what we think about. It may seem contrary to the idea of not being in control of what enters our mind, but it is not. A closer observation of the choice of words reveals that what we do have control over is what we choose to "fix" our thoughts on. When we do so, we are, in effect, "taking every thought captive to obey Christ." This practice can completely transform the life of any person.

Nothing can manifest in our lives without first passing through our thoughts. They are like a gateway to bring what is in the invisible realm into full manifestation in the natural realm. A thought can build, and a thought can destroy.

---

[92] Proverbs 23:7
[93] Philippians 4:8

If we examine the nature of God, who created all things, we see Him speaking creation into existence. This is not possible, unless what He desired to create was first a thought. If we are made in His image, then we also possess the capacity to speak what is first conceived in our thoughts. If King Solomon is correct in saying, "The tongue has the power of life and death, and those who love it will eat its fruit"[94] then it is also safe to conclude that this same life and death exist also in our thoughts. The man who commits the dastardliest acts in our society first conceived the notion in his thoughts. The man who sinned thought about it first.

James rightly says, when you are being tempted, do not say, "God is tempting me." God is never tempted to do wrong, and He never tempts anyone else. Temptation comes from our own desires, which entice us and drag us away.[95]

How do our desires entice us? How are we dragged away by our own lust? This is speaking about what is happening in the mind. What we see in our

---

[94] Proverbs 18:21
[95] James 1:13-14

thoughts entices us, and we make a conscious decision to manifest it.

To live a godly life then, we must be able to adequately differentiate between carnal and godly thoughts.

Every believer struggles with sinful or negative thoughts. There are times we have absolutely no control over the thoughts that enter our mind, simply because the receiver of thoughts is an open system to all creation. We can, however, control our thoughts. If we want to live a godly life in this world, it becomes mandatory that we learn to control the thoughts that flow through our hearts, and out through our mouth.

There are two types of mindsets, really. Either we are carnally minded, or spiritually minded. There is no middle ground. The quality of our lives will depend on which is more dominant. Paul says to be carnally minded is death, but to be spiritually minded is life and peace. Because the carnal mind is enmity against God: for it is not subject to the law of God, neither indeed can be. So then, they that are in the flesh cannot please God.[96]

To be carnally minded is to be in the flesh, and this mindset is enmity against God. What this means is that a carnally minded person dislikes God, and anything relating to spirituality, resulting in spiritual death, which is living a life separated from God and His laws and principles. This can also lead to early physical death. On the opposite side of the spectrum, a spiritually minded person pleases God and can lead a life of peace. Such a one will experience a good life and peace, which should be the desire of us all.

To be carnally minded means to cater to the appetites and impulses of one's sinful nature, which is displeasing to God. Carnally minded is thinking and doing what is right in one's own eyes. To be carnally minded means to be facts-minded, sense-ruled, emotions-driven, and controlled by sin, demonic influences, and natural circumstances. To be carnally minded means our thought process is generally what we can naturally expect in our fallen

---

[96] Romans 8:6-8

nature. It means our mindset is contrary to God and His Word, His will for our life, and His planned outcome for us in any situation. To the carnal mind, the Word of God is not reasonable. The carnal mind is always focused on the facts and focused on the problems only getting bigger and always there is little to no way out! Carnal mindset is always what we naturally can expect in our fallenness, which isn't much or too little too late. Carnal minded thinkers are always victims and never victors.[97]

One who is spiritually minded, however, is conscious of God, and is being led by the Holy Spirit instead of being guided by reasoning. One who entertains godly thoughts has their mind set on God's Word and craves God's nature and purposes for their lives. They are never satisfied with anything less than God's perfect will for their lives. Godly thoughts lead to nourishment through intimacy with God and meditating on God's word.

---

[97] The Difference Between Carnal Mindset & Spiritual Mindset. http://godswordalive.com/fact_truth_6. [Accessed on June 25, 2017]

David says, as the hart pants after the water brooks, so pants my soul after thee, O God. My soul is thirsty for God, for the living God.[98]

Jeremiah adds, "Thy words were found, and I did eat them; and thy word was unto me the joy and rejoicing of mine heart."[99]

To think godly thoughts, means we hand over the mind to the Holy Spirit, allowing Him to control our thinking. Every thought then is filtered through Him before it becomes a thought for us.

Paul sums it up nicely when he says, and let the peace (soul harmony which comes) from Christ rule (act as umpire continually) in your hearts (deciding and settling with finality all questions that arise in your minds, in that peaceful state) to which as (members of Christ's) one body you were also called (to live).[100]

Godly thoughts allow us to have the mindset of victory, so that every problem or frightening detail

---

[98] Psalm 42:1-2 - KJV
[99] Jeremiah 15:16
[100] Colossians 3:15

that seems stacked against us will lose its hold on our thinking. We will not be influenced by cultural norms or debates about class, race, or religion. Godly thoughts lead to an overabundance of love, peace, joy, patience, kindness, goodness, gentleness, faithfulness, and self-control, which is the fruit of the Spirit. Through the process of godly thinking we are empowered or activated to produce this fruit.

Even in the Church we have relied on our intellect and human reasoning and have been sense-driven rather than living out of our spirit. This has closed off the Holy Spirit speaking to us through our spirit regarding what to do with all the facts and circumstances weighed against us each day. We have missed out on revelation knowledge and discernment by our spirit through our spiritual senses.

We are either being carnally minded or spiritually minded because there is no in between. You either have the mindset of the natural, carnal world and you are facts-concentrated and reasoning-prone, resulting in natural expectations, or you give place to the mindset of the spirit, which is based on the truth of God's Word, and your expectations are supernatural, coming from a higher dimension or the heavenly realm. [101]

We should practice casting down imaginations, and every high thing that exalts itself against the knowledge of God, bringing into captivity every thought to the obedience of Christ.[102]

Carnal Thoughts

Carnal thinking is ruled by the senses and is enmity against God and His Word. The word "enmity" means extreme hatred. To think carnally is to have a strong hatred for God. This could be why we sometimes feel that God is miles away from us when we need Him the most. We often choose natural solutions to our situations because it seems to make perfect sense. We are trained to think this way from childhood. Natural, common sense does not make spiritual sense. Carnal thinking may force us to reject God, even after praying and confessing the Word of God. If we choose to be carnally minded

[101] The Difference Between Carnal Mindset & Spiritual Mindset. http://godswordalive.com/fact_truth_6. [Accessed on June 25, 2017]
[102] 2 Corinthians 10:5

after seeking God, it will nullify our prayers and dull our confessions of faith.

Carnal thoughts vex our spirit, which was designed to know God and be led by the Spirit of God. When we lean towards our own reasoning and humanistic ideas, we cannot expect to live a spirit-led life; thus, we miss out on the supernatural and righteousness, peace, and joy that we could enjoy in the Holy Spirit.

Carnal thoughts render our faith inoperative, and destroys it, making us unable to please God. It is impossible to please God without faith. Anyone who wants to come to Him must believe that God exists and that He rewards those who sincerely seek Him.[103]

Carnal thoughts will continually echo that God will not hear us, and He is not going to reward us. The carnal mindset reasons away what is rightful ours in Christ Jesus, for it just doesn't sound reasonable. This reasoning keeps us running to the world for our health care. Human, natural reasoning is why the Church, with the rest of the world, is so dependent

---

[103] Hebrews 11:6

on the Babylonian financial world system to borrow money. Therefore, we run to the world and we don't see demonstrations of Kingdom health care and Kingdom provision. We just can't mix the two kingdoms and expect to get Kingdom of God results. The Church must have clarity on this![104]

Carnal thoughts allow us to peer at reality behind the lens of the flesh. We must learn to replace our carnal thoughts with godly thoughts.

Godly Thoughts

Wholesome thought patterns and the impact of mature models are building blocks of godly behavior.[105]

We must guard our thought patterns, as they influence our behavior. Mark Twain wrote, "What a wee little part of a person's life are his acts and his

[104] The Difference Between Carnal Mindset & Spiritual Mindset. http://godswordalive.com/fact_truth_6. [Accessed on June 25, 2017]

[105] Luter, A. B., Jr. (1995). Philippians. In *Evangelical Commentary on the Bible* (Vol. 3, pp. 1046–1047). Grand Rapids, MI: Baker Book House.

words! His real life is led in his head, and is known to none but himself. All day long, the mill of his brain is grinding, and his thoughts, not those other things, are his history."[106]

We can only discern someone's thought process by what they do. Mark Twain's words can be modified to say that our thought life will form the basis for and is largely revealed in what we do and what we say. Our thought life composes a major part of who we are.

Jonathan Edwards says, "The ideas and images in men's minds are the invisible powers that constantly govern them."[107] It becomes imperative to bring our thought life into submission to Jesus Christ, thereby, living out our godly thoughts.

Paul gives us a starting point for developing godly thoughts. The list is as follows: Whatsoever things are: True, Noble, Right, Pure, Lovely, Admirable, Excellent, or Praiseworthy. It just so happens that seven is God's perfect number, and the number signifying rest. It is no surprise then that this practice

---

[106] (*Reader's Digest* [1/93], p. 155
[107] Source Unknown

would lead to peace for our souls, and rest in God. Paul is not emphasizing positive thinking, as some interpret this text to mean. What he exhorts is God-centered thinking, with a focus on God, not self. Positive thinking was developed from the Science of Mind and is contradictory in some sense to what Paul is trying to teach us. A Christian's thought life should be focused primarily on the great truth embedded in Scripture.

Whatever Is True

God cannot lie. What He has spoken is the only final test for truth. Even Jesus said, "I am the way, and the truth and the life."[108]

As fallen creatures, we are prone to the devil's lies and deception. The only way to avoid such deception is to know the truth. We should be so full of God's Word that there is no room for deception; we should automatically pass everything through the grid of God's Word. We must also avoid the pragmatism of our culture that tries to define and determine what is true.

---

[108] John 14:6

Whatever Is Honorable (Noble)

That which is honorable, or noble, inspires awe or reverence. It is dignified and worthy of respect. Paul listed this among the qualifications of deacons. Also, elders are admonished to keep their children under control "with all dignity." All believers are called upon to lead a quiet life with godliness and dignity.

Whatever Is Right

The word "right" stems from the word "righteous." We are called to be righteous people. John says, "Little children, let no one deceive you; the one who practices righteousness is righteous, just as He is righteous; the one who practices sin is of the devil."[109] To think right is to think on the nature of God, specifically as revealed in the person of Jesus. We should model our behavior after Him.

Whatever Is Pure

This particularly refers to keeping our bodies free from defilement by abstaining from sexual

---

[109] 1 John 3:7-8

immorality. Paul says, "I plead with you to give your bodies to God because of all He has done for you. Let them be a living and holy sacrifice — the kind He will find acceptable. This is truly the way to worship him."[110] Paul also pens a warning, "But do not let immorality or any impurity or greed even be named among you, as if proper among saints; and there must be no filthiness and silly talk, or coarse jesting, which are not fitting, but rather giving of thanks. For this you know with certainty, that no immoral or impure person or covetous man, who is an idolater, has an inheritance in the kingdom of Christ and God."[111]

Whatever Is Lovely

"Lovely" suggests what is agreeable, pleasing, and attractive. Sometimes, evil may appear attractive. We don't sin because we don't want to. Sin is attractive, but I would want to believe that the person of Jesus Christ is inherently attractive, and worthy of our consistent thought process.

---

[110] Romans 12:1
[111] Ephesians 5:3-5

Whatever Is of Good Repute

A "good repute" is to speak well of something. According to Paul, love always believes and sees the best in other people. It will never believe and accept an evil report, until evidence establishes such. We must also train ourselves to speak well of people, especially when we are not in their company.

If there be any virtue, if there be any praise — think on these things.

Solomon writes, "Watch over your heart with all diligence, for from it flows the springs of life."[112]

Frank Outlaw wrote, "Watch your thoughts, they become your words; watch your words, they become actions; watch your actions, they become habits; watch your habits, they become character; watch your character, for it becomes your destiny."

---

[112] Proverbs 4:23

Chapter 6
The Will of Man

Everything we have talked about to this point culminates in this very powerful characteristic of a human being called the "will." God chooses not to override this powerful trait embedded in man, neither can demons override it. It is said that even with satanists, the will of man causes a lot of trouble for demons.

It is here, in the will, that the choice is made and executed to fix our thoughts on what Paul recommends. It is here that we decide to desist from gossiping and choose to speak well of people, especially in their absence. It is here that we decide what declarations are uttered from our lips; we choose as an act of will to speak or be silent. Without the active participation of the will of man, a person is unable to move from the kingdom of darkness into the kingdom of light. It is an act of our will to live out the precepts of God and walk in His Spirit. It is also an act of man's will to deny His very existence, even in the face of insurmountable evidence.

It is widely believed that the will of man is embedded in the soul; but if this was true, then it doesn't clarity why a soul cannot get saved unless a man wills it. This would suggest that the will is independent of the soul and acts as a trading agent between what is accepted and what is rejected.

To say, "we have a choice" is neither a cliché nor an understatement. The full ramifications of such a human capacity is yet undiscovered, highly misunderstood, and profoundly underestimated. This is one area I encourage you not to underestimate yourself.

Many ministries are built on suppressing a man's will, but there is liberty coming to the house of God, and for the body of Christ in this age.

Our Will to Obey God

The life of Jesus is a good study in understanding how our will should function with God's will. When He was in the garden of Gethsemane, He made a very profound prayer: "Father, if you are willing, remove this cup from me. Nevertheless, not my will, but yours be done."[113]

As much as we might not want to admit it, Jesus had a will that was independent of the Father. It was clear in His prayer that His will was to escape the cup of wrath He was about to face, but within that single moment, He also made a conscious choice. He decided to attach His will to the will of the Father, thereby uniting them for a common cause. In that moment, Jesus surrendered His own will.

Interestingly, the same thing is said of the Holy Spirit: "When the Spirit of truth comes, he will guide you into all truth. He will not speak on his own, but will tell you what he has heard. He will tell you about the future."[114]

---

[113] Luke 22:42
[114] John 16:13

105

The text, "He will not speak on his own" suggests that He can choose to speak of His own free will. There is a distinction made that while the three are One, there are separate characteristics of each member of the Godhead.

Surrendering one's own will allows man to walk in obedience to God. It is not always easy to follow God while embracing one's own personal will, especially in matters of great difficulty.

The secret to success is to love God totally. Such love will be shown by obeying His law. God urges Joshua to obey the law of Moses carefully—like a straight path, from which it is dangerous to stray. The law is to govern his speech, thought, and behavior. If Joshua obeys God's law, then he will be prosperous and successful.[115]

The question has been asked for centuries, "If God is sovereign and He has our lives planned out to the finest details, then where does our free will fit in?" God never compels anyone to obey Him. It is an act

[115] Knowles, A. (2001). *The Bible guide* (1st Augsburg books ed., pp. 106–107). Minneapolis, MN: Augsburg.

of our will both to obey and to love God. In addition, there may not be such a thing as "free will."

The Bible says much more about the will of God than man's will, and what it does say is unsystematic. A believer can will to do what is right or what is wrong. Will may be more of an expression of oneself through the other facets of his personality rather than a distinct faculty in and of itself. These are the facets of the immaterial part of man through which he may glorify himself or glorify and serve his Lord.[116]

Paul says human beings are born "slaves" to sin. The choice of word there suggests that we have no choice in the matter, rendering us incapable of progressing beyond our sinful nature on our own accord. But then, through faith, God has delivered us from sin and has drafted us into a right relationship with Jesus Christ, so now we have shifted from being slaves to sin, to becoming slaves of righteousness.

---

[116] Ryrie, C. C. (1999). *Basic Theology: A Popular Systematic Guide to Understanding Biblical Truth* (pp. 228–229). Chicago, IL: Moody Press.

While we have a will to make our own choices, it is not a "free" will so to speak, because our nature determines our choices. We are only free to make choices consistent with our nature. When we are in sin, our will cannot free us from that sin, but our will functions in its capacity to put our faith in God and what He has done for us, thereby shifting our very nature so we can participate in divinity. The quality of our lives now depends on our will to choose to obey God, or choose to disobey.

As our own will is by nature totally corrupt, so God's will is only good. As little as we can of ourselves renounce our own will, so little can we subject our hearts to the will of God. Therefore, we are to pray: Grant unto us, give us strength that we may obey thy will.[117]

Our Will to Disobey God

It is a strange phenomenon, but the same effort expelled in obedience to God is the same that is required to disobey. The rationale for disobedience

---

[117] Thelemann, O. (1896). *An Aid to the Heidelberg Catechism.* (M. Peters, Trans.) (p. 428). Reading, PA: James I. Good, D. D, Publisher.

may seem easier to bear, but we should not fall to the delusion that one is easier than the other. Both carries cosmic repercussions that will either enhance lives or destroy. Of course, the most suitable conclusion is that a man should obey God. Yet, this is not the reality within the kingdom or outside of it. Is there really anything that can be said to convince humanity to walk in obedience to God by default? I doubt it. We can just examine the life experiences of a few people and see what we can glean from their lives.

The canon of Scripture barely makes it through the first three chapters before we see the immergence of disobedience coming from the heart of man. A serpent, the craftiest beast among them at the time, approached the woman and beguiled her into disobeying a direct command from God not to eat from a particular tree. She was tempted with the possibility of becoming "like God," which I find to be a strange allurement, considering previous chapters of Genesis stated they were made in the "image and likeness" of God. Could it be that they bore the image, but not yet the likeness? Surely, she could not have been tempted by what she already possessed.

So, the woman ate, and she in turn gave to her husband and he also ate. The Bible makes a startling statement: it was not Adam who was deceived by satan. The woman was deceived, and sin was the result.[118]

While Eve acted from her will, it was from a place of deception. Adam willfully choose to disobey and sin entered humanity. From a purely scientific perspective, one spoon of semen carries millions of sperm cells, each with a distinct mark and possibility of becoming a unique human being. This is the nature of reproduction. Essentially, Adam carried all human race in his loins, and his sin of disobedience affected every human being that would be born. We should be mindful that our willful choices don't just affect the guilty parties.

We move on to Adam and Eve's first two sons: Cain and Abel. One day, a sacrifice was required. Cain brought goods from his field, and Abel selected the best from his animals and brought it to God. Abel's sacrifice was accepted and Cain's rejected. The

---

[118] 1 Timothy 2:15

specific reason is not clear, and there is no point in speculating.

After God speaks with Cain about sin crouching at his door, Cain invites his brother out to the field, and commits pre-meditated murder. This was not a manslaughter case stemming from being seduced or provoked, neither was it self-defense. Cain made a conscious decision to kill his brother, and he suffered the consequences for his actions. This is the second time we see someone being expelled from the presence of God.

Let's examine a less consequential example: Saul and his son Jonathan are successful army commanders, driving back Israel's enemies. But there are two occasions when Saul offends God greatly. The first is when he offers a sacrifice without waiting for Samuel. In so doing he usurps the work of a priest and treats the sacrifice as a token of good luck. On another occasion Saul disobeys God by failing to totally destroy the Amalekites. He makes the excuse that he is saving the Amalekite cattle for sacrifices. But Samuel points out that it is more important to do what God wants: Does the Lord delight in burnt offerings and sacrifices as much as in obeying the voice of the Lord?[119]

King Saul makes a conscious decision of his will to disobey God on two occasions, costing him his reign as king. He lost his anointing, his kingdom, and eventually his life because of the choices he made.

The concern we have today is, "How do we obey God when we don't even know His will for our lives?" A good place to start is with the Word. In my book, *If You Love Me, Keep My Commandments*, I cite 613 verses in the New Testament that could be considered a command. Interestingly, that is the exact number of commandments under the Old Covenant.

The Will to Blame

After Adam and Eve fall to sin, God visits them. When He finds Adam and Eve, a very interesting conversation ensues: He answered, "I heard you in the garden, and I was afraid because I was naked; so I hid."

---

[119] Knowles, A. (2001). *The Bible guide* (1st Augsburg books ed., p. 137). Minneapolis, MN: Augsburg.

And he said, "Who told you that you were naked? Have you eaten from the tree that I commanded you not to eat from?"

The man said, "The woman you put here with me — she gave me some fruit from the tree, and I ate it."

Then the Lord God said to the woman, "What is this you have done?"

The woman said, "The serpent deceived me, and I ate."

So the Lord God said to the serpent, "Because you have done this, "Cursed are you above all livestock and all wild animals! You will crawl on your belly and you will eat dust all the days of your life. And I will put enmity between you and the woman, and between your offspring and hers; he will crush your head, and you will strike his heel."[120]

Only the animal (serpent) did not cast a blame on anyone. It would seem that casting blame is a human propensity. When God confronted Adam, who

---

[120] Genesis 3:10-15

knows all things, why didn't he just speak the truth? If Adam could stand before God and blame his actions on another, how much more we who stand accountable before mere men?

If our will can empower us to cast blame on others, it can also enable us to stand accountable for our actions. It comes with practice.

Man's Corrupted Will

The will of man has fallen and become corrupted, with an inability to determine what is good and acceptable in God's sight. Thomas Boston wrote, "The natural man's will is in satan's fetters, hemmed in within the circle of evil, and cannot move beyond it, any more than a dead man can raise himself out of his grave." We have lost the power to choose, to act, and to pursue that which is good. Paul says it this way: I do not understand what I do. For what I want to do I do not do, but what I hate I do. And if I do what I do not want to do, I agree that the law is good. As it is, it is no longer I myself who do it, but it is sin living in me. For I know that good itself does not dwell in me, that is, in my sinful nature. For I have the desire to do what is good, but I cannot carry

114

it out. For I do not do the good I want to do, but the evil I do not want to do—this I keep on doing. Now if I do what I do not want to do, it is no longer I who do it, but it is sin living in me that does it.[121]

This is the propensity of a corrupted will, not yet fully redeemed, not yet fully surrendered. It is the struggle of us all as believers, how to bend our will to do what God wants and not what we want. But then, Paul offers a solution: "I die daily."[122] It is the "I" in my WILL that needs to die and surrender to the "I AM."

Consistent with his denial of any such moral corruption of nature as the theory of original sin implied, Pelagius asserted the full and unimpaired freedom of the will. He maintained that all men are governed by their own will. Man brings into the world with him the capacity for good and evil. We are created without virtue and so also without vice. In his letter to Demetrias, Pelagius unhesitatingly disclaims any idea of moral inability or weakness in the attainment of goodness. "We contradict the Lord when we say, it is hard: it is difficult: we cannot: we

---

[121] Romans 7:15-20
[122] 1 Corinthians 15:31

are men: we are encompassed with mortal flesh. O unholy audacity. We charge God with a twofold ignorance, that He does not seem to know what He has made, nor what He has commanded: just as if, forgetting the human weakness of which He Himself is the author, He had imposed laws on man which He cannot endure." Elsewhere (*De lib. Arbitrio*, as quoted by Augustine, *De Gratia Christi*, c. 4) he distinguishes three things, to be able, to will, and to be, *posse, velle, esse.* To be able; to place in nature: to will, in free will, to be, *i.e.,* to do, in the effect. The first refers peculiarly to God who has bestowed this on His creature; the other two must be referred to men, because they flow from the fountain of free will.[123]

We can be free from a corrupt, unrenewed will and experience a full renewal of our will. After all, Jesus did come to restore that which was lost, broken, and marred. He came to make all things new.

---

[123] Ince, W. (1877–1887). Pelagius (2). In W. Smith & H. Wace (Eds.), *A Dictionary of Christian Biography, Literature, Sects and Doctrines* (Vol. 4, p. 294). London: John Murray.

Man's Renewed Will

Since you have heard about Jesus and have learned the truth that comes from Him, throw off your old sinful nature and your former way of life, which is corrupted by lust and deception. Instead, let the Spirit renew your thoughts and attitudes.[124]

The renewal of a man's thoughts and will is a work of the Holy Spirit within the believer. Understand this profound but interesting fact: Regarding our redemption, God choose to do all the hard work. All He left for us to do is believe and receive.

_____

[124] Ephesians 4:21-23

117

Chapter 7

Renewing and Transforming the Spirit, Soul, and Mind

Our present form of existence is not what God intended for us when He said, "Let us make man." We need to understand that there was an original intention: a form and body and pattern of existence that Adam and Eve enjoyed before choosing to disobey God. I believe we lost more than we could ever imagine in that fall.

Christian Mystics believe that we lived in a completely different realm but fell to the lowest dimensions when we sinned. We fell to the same level of the animals and became far less in structure and function than God originally had in mind. If we

119

are ever to become what we were meant to become, there needs to be a transformation of Spirit, Soul, Mind, and Body.

Christians think that the change is supposed to come after death, but if this were true, then death would be our salvation and not Jesus. If Jesus indeed is our salvation, the Restorer of all things, the One who has come to make all things new, then the transformation must begin now. Consciously and Subconsciously, I believe we are being transformed. For Christ is the visible image of the invisible God. He existed before anything was created and is supreme over all creation.[125] For those God foreknew he also predestined to be conformed to the image of his Son, that he might be the firstborn among many brothers and sisters.[126]

We are being changed from faith to faith, and from glory to glory. Most of us don't know the process we are walking through and we think it is somewhere in the future, when it is actually now, and the first aspect of humanity that should be addressed is our minds.

---

[125] Colossians 1:15
[126] Romans 8:29

To the Hebrew way of thinking, there is no distinctive terminology for the conception of the mind. To the Greek world, the mind plays a very important role in man's understanding. In the Old Testament, there was no separate word used for a man's mind. Translators of the English versions have supplied other words (soul, spirit, or heart) as the context dictates. Thus, precise distinctions between these terms are hard to define. Generally, one might say that a man in his totality is a soul but he has a spirit and a heart. These terms may represent his mind. This means that the widely held distinction between the mind as the seat of thinking and the heart as the seat of feeling is alien to the meaning these terms carry in the Old Testament.[127]

It is believed among the scientific community that the space between thought and emotions is almost non-existent. Those who suffer from anxiety know there is no gap between a dreadful thought and the dreadful emotion that accompanies it. They are so close that one may even believe that the emotion came before the thought. If emotions are linked to

---

[127] Elwell, W. A., & Beitzel, B. J. (1988). Mind. In *Baker encyclopedia of the Bible* (Vol. 2, p. 1461). Grand Rapids, MI: Baker Book House.

desires, and God cares about our desires, then it is safe to say that we need to address our thought patterns.

Thoughts do not originate in the brain. There is no scientific proof to support that claim. Our mind is in our hearts. Essentially, scientists say that only 10% of our brain functions, and that is the maximum attributed to geniuses. Regular people function at less. If we can accomplish some of the things we have done in the last few centuries at such a low brain function, what if our brains were functioning at 100% or close? Surely Adam knew this level of functionality as a human, but none of us do. Not yet.

The question to ask is not, "Why should we renew the Spirit, Soul, and Mind" but "Why not?" When faced with limitations, we have often said, "I am only human," but this is not very accurate, is it? To be "truly human" is to have our brain capacity functioning at 100%. To be "truly human" is to understand how Adam could traverse worlds, name every existing animal on the planet, see into heaven, and hear the voice of God walking in a garden. The suggestion here is, that is who we are.

Let's say we completely lost our identity in God and begun to attach ourselves to a far less level of existence. Jesus came to address that. John now says, "As he is, so also are we in this world."[128] The only people I have heard use this Scripture are those in the Christian mystical movement. From a traditional, mental perspective, how does one compare themselves to a human being who walked on water, walked through walls, changed the genetic structure of water into wine, cast out demons with a breath and healed all who came to Him for healing? How can we ever understand our true identity in God, through the prototype Jesus Christ, unless we begin to be transformed?

The answer is quite simple. We need to be transformed so we can disconnect ourselves from the identity of limitations, restraint, and powerlessness, and be reconnected to God, and our true self.

There are several things we can do at the very basic level that will aid in the transformative process. As we put some of these into practice, it will not just

---

[128] 1 John 4:17

transform our Spirit, Soul, and Mind, but it will begin to change our DNA and how our brain functions.

Dr. Caroline Leaf is one of the leading Christian Neuroscientists who believes that addressing the mind will transform the whole person at a molecular, submolecular, and spiritual level. She writes, "Rest in the assurance that what God has enabled you to do with your mind is more powerful and effective than any medication, any threat, any sickness, or any neurological challenge. Research shows that 75–98% of all mental, physical, and behavioral illness is caused by our thought life. Every thought changes and is shaping our DNA. We have countless variations of genes that can switch on or off depending on our thoughts and lifestyle. Toxic thoughts switch off DNA codes that lead to healing and turn on genes that may be predisposed to a disease or illness. Positive thoughts switch on genes that heal and override any "bad genes." Our genetic makeup is fluctuating by the minute based on what we are thinking and choosing. Toxic thoughts act as a signal that interrupts normal gene expression, keeping you healthy."[129]

We have the power to rewire our beliefs, habits, and mindsets and program them into our brain, thereby, creating new pathways that will inevitably cause us to function differently as citizens of another world.

Receive Salvation

Therefore, if anyone is in Christ, the new creation has come: The old has gone, the new is here![130] In order to change our position, and get in Christ, we must confess with our mouth the Lord Jesus and believe in our heart that God has raised Him from the dead, then we will be saved.

A Rabbi, Nicodemus, once approached Jesus by night to question Him about this process. Jesus told him, "I assure you, no one can enter the Kingdom of God without being born of water and the Spirit."[131] Nicodemus thought Jesus was initially referring to

---

[129] Switch on Your Brain by Dr. Caroline Leaf. https://renewingallthings.com/spiritual-health/switch-brain-dr-caroline-leaf/ [Accessed on June 26, 2017]
[130] 1 Corinthians 5:17
[131] John 3:5

being born again of a natural mother, so Jesus had to make it plain, and even then, many still argue today concerning what Jesus meant by being born of the "water and the Spirit."

We receive salvation by believing in Jesus Christ, who has become our salvation; our redemption; our source of renewal. Yet, it's not a renewal as a refurbishing of an old house, but a removal of what was there, replacing it with something new, something better.

Meditate on Scriptures

Meditation is an excellent way to activate the power of God's Word in our lives. The idea is to internalize Scripture so the Holy Spirit can work through it to guide us, teach us, and purify us. There are more explicit references to meditation in the Bible than to memorization, probably because meditation usually assumes memorization. God himself commands meditation and explains its benefit: "Keep this Book of the Law always on your lips; meditate on it day and night, so that you may be careful to do everything written in it. Then you will be prosperous and successful."[132] In context, the benefits are *not* that Joshua will be rich and famous, but rather that he will be obedient to God's commands and successfully complete what God called him to do—that is, he will be successful in God's eyes.[133]

Nobody taught better on this practice than King David. Psalm 119 is replete with admonition to meditate on the Word, and the power of this practice.

I will meditate on Your precepts and regard Your ways. I shall delight in Your statutes; I shall not forget Your word.[134] My eyes anticipate the night watches, That I may meditate on Your word.[135] Your word I have treasured in my heart, That I may not sin against You.[136]

---

[132] Joshua 1:8

[133] Aaron, D. (2012). *Understanding Your Bible in 15 Minutes a Day* (p. 177). Minneapolis, MN: Bethany House Publisher.

[134] Psalm 119:15-16

[135] Psalm 119:148

[136] Psalm 119:11

Some traditional Christians believe "meditation" to be a new age word and practice, yet the word is repeated so many times in Scripture, that it is hard to ignore. We can literally encounter God while meditating on Scripture. Jesus says, "I am the door."[137] John says, "The Word became flesh and dwelt among us."[138] If Jesus is the Word, then the Word is a door. The function of a door is not to be merely observed but used to access other realms and dimensions. When we make a conscious, intentional choice to meditate on the Word of God, we can use the Scriptures to encounter God. We will experience more of His love, come into a better understanding of truth, and know Him more intimately. All it takes is, at least, thirty minutes a day.

Praying the Word

Maybe a more fitting definition of this practice is "make declarations," not just once, or occasionally, but consistently, several times a day. When you pray, don't babble on and on as people of other religions do. They think their prayers are answered

---

[137] John 10:9
[138] John 1:14

merely by repeating their words again and again.[139] Notice it says, "their words." I don't think the same applies to God's Word because even the word "meditation" denotes chewing the cud like a cow. There is a lot of repetition at work in the act of a cow feeding itself. In addition, we are told to, "Put me in remembrance: let us plead together: declare you, that you may be justified."[140]

There has been an upsurge of revelations released in the last few decades about a lot of things where misconception and misinterpretation was apparently prevalent. One such example is God responding to Job. It is now becoming widely accepted that the questions God asked Job was within his capacity to perform as a man, yet Job did not seem to be aware of this knowledge. It can make such a big difference when revelation comes about who we are. For example, God asked Job, "Have you ever commanded the morning to appear and caused the dawn to rise in the east?"[141] It was not a suggestion that Job was incapable, but that he had

---

[139] Matthew 6:7
[140] Isaiah 43:26
[141] Job 38:12

failed to do the very basic things that a human being was created to do.

Declarations are good for the wee hours of the morning. We should also practice reading the Bible aloud because, "…faith comes from hearing, and hearing through the word of Christ."[142] There is no way of escaping repetition when it comes to Scripture.

Biblical Reframing

The Word of God is eternal and true, and it is completely sufficient in offering all we need to know God, ourselves, and the lives we are called to live. So we can tailor our lives to fit the word of God, and for most believers, this is referred to as reframing our lives. It is a practical step in the transformative process that may take great effort to master and adequately implement, but it will be worth the effort and sacrifice it demands.

To reframe is to take a new perspective and apply it over the old. It is not an attempt to pour old wine

---

[142] Romans 10:17

into new bottles, or new wine into old bottles. We are very aware of the catastrophe that would cause. Whatever the Scripture teaches, in a practical sense, will undoubtedly override some old mindsets. It is naturally expected that we release the old for the new. Some call this unlearning and relearning, but the process is actually a little more technical. We will often try to force the new to fit the old because we are hesitant to release that which we have grown accustomed to. But reframing demands that we do. What most of us do is try to force Scripture to fit our comfort level, which causes us to sidestep or blatantly avoid more than 90% of Scripture, because then it doesn't make sense in the context of our limited knowledge.

A lot of us have created our own "god" that we worship. We all have an idea of who we think He is, how He operates, how He thinks, and the day-to-day decisions He is making in relation to humanity. But can a fish in the sea know the full extent of the body of water that he has found himself in? Does the fish even know where he is, in relation to the whole body of ocean? Fish can only know as much of the sea as that which forms the environment around him. In a similar way, we must never assume from our limited vantage point that we know God, to the point that when we are faced with something new, we try to fit it into what we already know, thereby, rendering ourselves unteachable.

Let's give an example. Paul says about us, "I can do all things through Christ who strengthens me." This is a broad statement with only one apparent meaning, "We can do all things." We are accustomed to think that God can do all things, but we can't. Where does God dwell? Therefore, we need to revisit our vocabulary to remove the word "can't." Essentially, we are reframing both our mental capacity and our speech to fit what the Bible says about us. This is how we practice biblical reframing.

Biblical Self-Talk

There is no better example in Scripture of this practice than King David. When God breathed into Adam, he became a living soul. Jesus came to save our souls. So, our soul is a real, eternal person. This makes sense now when we study the very weird practices of this Biblical King who was constantly speaking to his soul:

132

Bless the LORD, O my soul: and all that is within me, bless his holy name. Bless the LORD, O my soul, and forget not all his benefits: Who forgives all thine iniquities; who heals all thy diseases; Who redeems thy life from destruction; who crowns thee with lovingkindness and tender mercies; Who satisfies thy mouth with good things; so that thy youth is renewed like the eagle's.[143] Why, my soul, are you downcast? Why so disturbed within me? Put your hope in God, for I will yet praise him, my Savior and my God.[144]

There is a song that says, "Speak over yourself; Encourage yourself—in the Lord." If Biblical self-talk is practiced, there would be less depression in our world. We must learn to speak to ourselves, speak the word of God over ourselves. If faith does come by hearing, then we need to speak the Word of God, especially as it relates to our identity, over ourselves until our soul believes it. This is actually a very powerful practice. What does the Word of God say about us:

---

[143] Psalm 103:1-5
[144] Psalm 43:5

Therefore, if anyone is in Christ, he is a new creation. The old has passed away; behold, the new has come.[145]

But you are a chosen race, a royal priesthood, a holy nation, a people for his own possession, that you may proclaim the excellencies of him who called you out of darkness into his marvelous light.[146]

For we are his workmanship, created in Christ Jesus for good works, which God prepared beforehand, that we should walk in them.[147]

There is therefore now no condemnation for those who are in Christ Jesus.[148]

But to all who did receive him, who believed in his name, he gave the right to become children of God.[149]

---

[145] 2 Corinthians 5:17
[146] 1 Peter 2:9
[147] Ephesians 2:10
[148] Romans 8:1
[149] John 1:12

For our sake he made him to be sin who knew no sin, so that in him we might become the righteousness of God.[150]

I am the vine; you are the branches. Whoever abides in me and I in him, he it is that bears much fruit, for apart from me you can do nothing.[151]

Or do you not know that your body is a temple of the Holy Spirit within you, whom you have from God? You are not your own.[152]

Little children, you are from God and have overcome them, for he who is in you is greater than he who is in the world.[153]

Evidence of Renewal

The mind must be renewed to conform to or apprehend the will of God. "Do not conform any longer to the pattern of the world, but be transformed by the renewing of your mind. Then

---

[150] 2 Corinthians 5:21
[151] John 15:5
[152] 1 Corinthians 6:19
[153] 1 John 4:4

you will be able to test and approve what God's will is."[154] Being made new in the attitude of our minds is similar in thrust. In each case, the issue is the discernment of God's will over and against an opposing and imposing mind-set. Renewal, which is related to conversion and regeneration by the Holy Spirit, is the prerequisite for reaching an understanding of God's will.[155]

An individual who has been renewed will experience several changes. The first most obvious is a change in speech. Paul says, "When I was a child, I talked like a child, I thought like a child, I reasoned like a child. When I became a man, I put the ways of childhood behind me."[156]

While Paul uses an example from the natural order of things, for example, a child, it has spiritual significance. Paul emphasizes growing up to spiritual maturity and is firm that believers shouldn't insist on living off baby food. It doesn't

---

[154] Romans 12:2

[155] Towner, P. H. (1996). Mind/Reason. In *Evangelical dictionary of biblical theology* (electronic ed., p. 529). Grand Rapids: Baker Book House.

[156] 1 Corinthians 13:11

contradict Jesus' admonition to become like a child. Jesus was referring to the unmovable faith of little ones. Paul spoke about three things: speech, thought, and reason. We have already established that speech stems from thoughts and reason expound thoughts. So, Paul was directly addressing how we think, because he goes further to say, "Be renewed in the spirit of your mind."[157]

The evidence that one has been renewed is a change in thinking, thereby, influencing a change in speech and reason. And finally, there will be a change in behaviors. One's mind cannot be renewed without dramatically affecting our actions. A renewed individual will act and speak different, reflecting the change that has happened in the mind within the heart.

The major benefit of being renewed and transformed is activation. One who has experienced transformation at any level now carries the anointing to activate that same level in the world around them.

---

[157] Ephesians 4:23

Whatever we learn to access, we can teach others to access as well. Whatever is given to us is not given so we can boast. Paul speaks about this: For by the grace given me I say to every one of you: Do not think of yourself more highly than you ought, but rather think of yourself with sober judgment, in accordance with the faith God has distributed to each of you. For just as each of us has one body with many members, and these members do not all have the same function, so in Christ we, though many, form one body, and each member belongs to all the others. We have different gifts, according to the grace given to each of us. If your gift is prophesying, then prophesy in accordance with your faith; if it is serving, then serve; if it is teaching, then teach; if it is to encourage, then give encouragement; if it is giving, then give generously; if it is to lead, do it diligently; if it is to show mercy, do it cheerfully.[158]

Transformation, renewal, and rewiring pulls us closer to being conformed to the image of Christ. It is not new, in a sense, but a restoration of original intent. It was God's intention for humanity before the derailment occurred because of sin.

---

[158] Romans 12:3-8

The whole purpose of the salvation experience is to restore original intent. We need to experience the full benefit of God's transforming power through His Holy Spirit so we can see this working in the lives of our children. We cannot achieve this by being passive, but we must be deliberate and intentional in what we are doing so we can experience the reality He has for us.

Conclusion

Jesus is not just our Savior, but a prototype. The Bible says about Him, "[He] is the image of the invisible God, the firstborn of every creature."[159] What this means is that Jesus was the model used when making man, and everything else. If man was indeed made in the image of God, and in His likeness, then all that Jesus is, we are.

We were born with the instinctive ability to be human. It is easy to be human. We eat, sleep, run, walk, laugh, dance, cry, fall in love, fall out of love, suffer, feel, think, breath, get sick, get well, get emotional, exercise, reason, learn, grow, have sex, reproduce, work, play, go to church, go to weddings, go to funerals, visit people in hospitals and prisons,

---

[159] Colossians 1:15

make money, spend money, and make more money. Our human lives are a never-ending cycle of these things from birth to death.

Being human is normal, natural, anybody can do it. Becoming like Jesus and partaking in God's divine nature—now that takes work.

I have heard so many testimonies of what a human being can do and can become, both from people I have met personally and others I have not met in person, that it is too much to record it all. I understand now John's statement that what Jesus did was too much to record, but enough was recorded that we might believe.

You don't need to hear everyone's story to believe. They all confirm one thing: what people had access to in Biblical times, in terms of their spiritual, supernatural, divine experiences, is available to us today. We have the same access.

As we consider our human-ness, we should remember we were created as an open system. We should avoid getting stuck in any aspect of our human nature. God is training us to be sons and daughters. Everything you are experiencing at this present moment has something to do with your training. Life is a perpetual classroom. You send your children to school to learn what they don't already know. There is never a point in your life when you stop learning. Greater knowledge and revelation is always waiting to be revealed. Transformation comes through learning. Many believers allow themselves to get stuck and start rejecting new knowledge when it comes. We become like a child, sitting in a classroom, telling the teacher that they don't know what they are talking about, or we are highly skeptical of the content. Our skepticism and fear blocks our spiritual growth and God's attempt to train us as sons and daughters is neutralized. We must remain open, which is why when something new is about to be taught, the teacher may ask us to keep an open mind. It doesn't matter what you are going through or what you are facing in life, this is your training. That is why Paul says, "All things work together for good."[160] If your personality causes you to get stuck and not allow yourself to grow in and through your experiences, you will react to people and things in the same way.

---

[160] Romans 8:28

Therefore, you will find yourself in a cycle as God keeps throwing the same things and people at you, until you learn to respond based on His divine nature in you.

The truth about you, if you can handle it, is that you are *not only human*, but Divinely Human. We cannot truly participate in God's divine nature unless we already possess the capacity to do so.

Bibliography

1. Bolman, L. G., & Deal, T. E. (2011). Leading with soul: An uncommon journey of spirit (Vol. 381). John Wiley & Sons.
2. Bosson, Christopher James. A scriptural appraisal of the necessary connection between progressive sanctification and compatibilist freedom. The Southern Baptist Theological Seminary, 2010.
3. Calkins, A. B. (1990). The Tripartite Biblical Vision of Man: A Key to the Christian Life. Doctor Communis, 43(2), 135-159.
4. Calkins, Arthur Burton. "The Tripartite Biblical Vision of Man: A Key to the Christian Life." Doctor Communis 43, no. 2 (1990): 135-159.
5. Clines, D. J. (1968). The image of God in man. Tyndale Bulletin, 19(53), 103.
6. Combs, William W. "Does the Believer Have One Nature or Two?" Detroit Baptist Seminary Journal 2 (1997): 81-103.

7. Crum, Ronnie J. Decision-making styles, leadership styles, and selected influences on decision-making. Assemblies of God Theological Seminary, 2014.
8. Daniel Tyler, Be Successful in Your Ministry I – The Doctrine of Man, Series 1 - Lecture 12, International Seminary (Florida) 1.
9. Diener, Ed, and Richard E. Lucas. 11 personality and subjective well-being. Edited by D. Kahneman, E. Diener, and N. Schwarz. New York, NY: Russell Sage, 1999.
10. Engelke, M. (2007). A problem of presence: Beyond scripture in an African church (Vol. 2). Univ. of California Press.
11. Greggo, Stephen P. "Counselor identity and Christian imagination: striving for professional case conceptualization and artistic contextualization." Journal of Psychology and Christianity 35, no. 1 (2016): 22-36.
12. Jimmie L. Chapman, Reborn and Transformed (Bible Believers Books, 2011), 118.
13. Köstenberger, A. J. (2002). Encountering John: The gospel in historical, literary, and theological perspective. Baker Academic.
14. Moreland, James Porter, and Scott B. Rae. Body & soul: Human nature & the crisis in ethics. InterVarsity Press, 2009.
15. Pinnock, Clark H. The grace of God, the will of man: a case for arminianism. Harper Collins, 1989.

16. Santini, Michael T., Systematic Theology III–Dr Bryan Burton, and Miguel Romero TA. "Dispensationalism and the Soteriology of Charles C. Ryrie."

17. Tozer, A. W. (2008). Man, the Dwelling Place of God: What it Means to Have Christ Living in You. Moody Publishers.

18. Underhill, E. (2015). Mysticism: A Study in the Nature and Development of Man's Spiritual Consciousness (Vol. 8). Aeterna Press.

19. Valsiner, Jaan. The guided mind: A sociogenetic approach to personality. Harvard University Press, 1998.

20. Vonier, A. (2002). A Key to the Doctrine of the Eucharist. Wipf and Stock Publishers.

21. Wilkinson, R. (2001). Rudolf Steiner: An Introduction to His Spiritual World-view, Anthroposophy. Temple Lodge Publishing.

22. Yorke, M. (2000). Eric Gill: man of flesh and spirit. Tauris Parke Paperbacks.

23. Manser, M.H. (2009). Dictionary of Bible Themes: The Accessible and Comprehensive Tool for Topical Studies. London: Martin Manser.

24. Robert C. Solomon, True to Our Feelings (Oxford University Press, 2007), 1.

25. Plato, Republic 4.14, &439C-D; Aristotle, Nichomanchean Ethics 7.3.7.

26. Seneca, On Anger 1.1-2, 2.4.1, 3.1.3-6.

27. The Emotions of Jesus by G. Walter Hansen. http://www.christianitytoday.com/ct/1997/februa ry3/7t2042.html. [Accessed on June 25, 2017]

28. Aaron, D. (2012). Understanding Theology in 15 Minutes a Day (p. 102). Minneapolis, MN: Bethany House Publishers.

29. Heyink, B. (2016). Joy. In J. D. Barry, D. Bomar, D. R. Brown, R. Klippenstein, D. Mangum, C. Sinclair Wolcott, … W. Widder (Eds.), The Lexham Bible Dictionary. Bellingham, WA: Lexham Press.

30. A General Theory of Emotion In Humans and Other Intelligences by Ben Goertzel. http://www.goertzel.org/dynapsyc/2004/Emotion s.htm. [Accessed on June 25, 2017]

31. The Complexity of Fear by Mary C. Lamia. https://www.psychologytoday.com/blog/intense-emotions-and-strong-feelings/201112/the-complexity-fear. [Accessed on June 25, 2017]

32. Elwell, W. A., & Beitzel, B. J. (1988). Mind. In Baker encyclopedia of the Bible (Vol. 2, p. 1461). Grand Rapids, MI: Baker Book House.

33. The Difference Between Carnal Mindset & Spiritual Mindset. http://godswordalive.com/fact_truth_6. [Accessed on June 25, 2017]

34. Luter, A. B., Jr. (1995). Philippians. In Evangelical Commentary on the Bible (Vol. 3, pp. 1046–1047). Grand Rapids, MI: Baker Book House.

148

35. Ince, W. (1877–1887). Pelagius (2). In W. Smith & H. Wace (Eds.), A Dictionary of Christian Biography, Literature, Sects and Doctrines (Vol. 4, p. 294). London: John Murray.

36. Ryrie, C. C. (1999). Basic Theology: A Popular Systematic Guide to Understanding Biblical Truth (pp. 228–229). Chicago, IL: Moody Press.

37. Thelemann, O. (1896). An Aid to the Heidelberg Catechism. (M. Peters, Trans.) (p. 428). Reading, PA: James I. Good, D. D, Publisher.

38. Knowles, A. (2001). The Bible guide (1st Augsburg books ed., p. 137). Minneapolis, MN: Augsburg.

39. Aaron, D. (2012). Understanding Your Bible in 15 Minutes a Day (p. 177). Minneapolis, MN: Bethany House Publisher.

40. Towner, P. H. (1996). Mind/Reason. In Evangelical dictionary of biblical theology (electronic ed., p. 529). Grand Rapids: Baker Book House.

41. Switch on Your Brain by Dr. Caroline Leaf. https://renewingallthings.com/spiritual-health/switch-brain-dr-caroline-leaf/ [Accessed on June 26, 2017]

42. Aaron, D. (2012). Understanding Your Bible in 15 Minutes a Day (p. 177). Minneapolis, MN: Bethany House Publisher.

43. Towner, P. H. (1996). Mind/Reason. In Evangelical dictionary of biblical theology (electronic ed., p. 529). Grand Rapids: Baker Book House.

44. Ryrie, C. C. (1999). Basic Theology: A Popular Systematic Guide to Understanding Biblical Truth (p. 287). Chicago, IL: Moody Press.

45. https://www.livescience.com/20380-particles-quantum-tunneling-timing.html

46. http://www.collective-evolution.com/2013/12/05/the-illusion-of-matter-our-physical-material-world-isnt-really-physical-at-all/

47. https://nwspiritism.com/spiritist-knowledge/our-physical-world-is-actually-created-by-thought/

48. http://johnassaraf.com/law-of-attraction/why-you-should-be-aware-of-quantum-physics-2

49. The Holy Bible: English Standard Version. (2016). (1 Co 15:44). Wheaton: Standard Bible Society.

50. Freeman, J. M., & Chadwick, H. J. (1998). Manners & customs of the Bible (pp. 314–315). North Brunswick, NJ: Bridge-Logos Publishers.

51. http://therisinglight.com/tag/transrelocation/

www.ingramcontent.com/pod-product-compliance
Lightning Source LLC
LaVergne TN
LVHW051241080426
835513LV00016B/1704